MRS ELIZABETH BARRY
(1658-1713)

To Lita,
Enjoy a bit of Barry
Love
Sue

Also by Susan Margaret Cooper:

THOMAS ALCOCK: A Biographical Account
"A Wonderful Insight into the Life of Thomas Alcock"
"Intriguing Subject, Beautifully Researched"

ELIZABETH MONTAGU COUNTESS OF SANDWICH
(1674-1757): Lord Rochester's Jacobite daughter who abandoned England for France
"A biography deviating from well-known figures to concentrate on Lord Rochester's daughter Elizabeth"

WILLIAM CLARKE ESQUIRE (1640-1688):
A Biographical Account
"Very impressive and detailed research"
"The interesting life of a late 17th century gentleman"

ROGER BRIDGWATER (1694-1754):
"An Old Actor & An Honest Man"
Richard Cross - Theatre Prompter - 1754
"A Very Informative Book for All Interested in the Theatre, Especially in the 18th Century"

SIR ANDREW BALFOUR, M.D. (1630-1694):
Governor & Companion to John Wilmot, 2nd Earl of Rochester 'The Grand Tour'

MRS ELIZABETH BARRY (1658-1713)

MUSINGS ON A RESTORATION ACTRESS

SUSAN MARGARET COOPER

Copyright © 2021 Susan Margaret Cooper

The moral right of the author has been asserted.

All rights reserved.

Apart from any fair dealing for the purposes of research or private study, or criticism or review, as permitted under the Copyright, Designs and Patents Act 1988, this publication may only be reproduced, stored or transmitted, in any form or by any means, with the prior permission in writing of the author, or in the case of reprographic reproduction in accordance with the terms of licences issued by the Copyright Licensing Agency.

For those who wish to read it

CONTENTS

INTRODUCTION

PART ONE
Musings on Mrs. Elizabeth Barry and Her Friends

PART TWO
Town Mills, Newbury

PART THREE
Gabriel Ballam's Family Roots

PART FOUR
Gabriel Ballam's Friends

EPILOGUE

INTRODUCTION

Elizabeth Barry by Charles Knight,
published by E. & S. Harding,
after Silvester (Sylvester) Harding,
after Sir Godfrey Kneller, Bt,
stipple engraving, published 17 December 1792.
© National Portrait Gallery, London.

Mrs. Elizabeth Barry, celebrated actress, lover of a few, of a supposedly dubious immoral mercenary reputation, mother to a least one, successful business woman, the list

MRS ELIZABETH BARRY (1658-1713)

goes on… However, it will be seen that at her untimely death in 1713 her close friends were people from many walks of life. And it is interesting to note that among her possessions, at the time of her death, there was a portrait of John Wilmot, 2nd Earl of Rochester, her ardent lover for a time and natural father of her daughter Elizabeth, 'little Barry'. That one piece of evidence surely belies her supposed indifference to the man, before and after his death in 1680, and proves to some extent that her fondness for Rochester endured for many years after their short affair began in the early 1670s. Two of Rochester's daughters also make an appearance in this work.

***

Having worked as a legal secretary for most of my life, and during that time for a good while in probate departments engrossing wills, the terminology has come in handy with my interest in historical research and with the inevitable transcribing of old wills. Such documents can reveal so much about the testators' families, friends and their trusted executors.

Having obtained a copy of the will of Mrs. Elizabeth Barry, I was fascinated to read who were her legatees. A good deal can be gleaned from the will regarding her circle of friends, who read like characters in a restoration play, and are as diverse as the many parts Barry herself played upon the London Stage: A gentleman; the son of a grocer from Southwark; a grandson of an Evesham vicar; a Mrs. Cary; a Mrs. Phubs; a famous actress; the wife of a Court artist; a gentleman, a former Page to the Prince of Denmark; and a young woman who became the wife of a Fleet Street publisher.

Introduction

The scene was set.

The most intriguing of these legatees was a Gabriel Ballam, gentleman, who was left a substantial legacy by Mrs. Barry; *an estate at Newbury consisting of mills.* What were these mills? Who had previously owned them? How long had they been in use? All questions that needed answers.

Although *an estate at Newbury consisting of mills* has often been alluded to with reference to Mrs. Barry's will, there was a distinct lack of detail as to when she obtained them, as to where these mills *were* in Newbury, or any evidence as to the their name.

Anyone who has read my works know that I specialize in researching hitherto hidden facts about historical characters, and my inquisitiveness as to Mrs. Barry's mills, and more, has led me to this work.

PART ONE

MUSINGS ON MRS. ELIZABETH BARRY AND HER FRIENDS

"If any thing be overlooked, or not accurately inserted, let no one find fault, but take into consideration that this history is compiled from all quarters." [From the title page of *Some Account of the English Stage...* 1832.]

Although this work is not a biography of the celebrated actress, it is appropriate that a short summary be included for anyone who is not familiar with her:

> "Mrs. Elizabeth Barry was buried in the parish church of Acton, in the south oyle, under the end of Madam Lamb's pew, being att the uper end between the two pillers; she was buried the 12th day of November 1713."—Elizabeth Barry was daughter of a gentleman of an ancient family and good estate, which was so much injured during the civil war, that his children were obliged to make their own fortunes. His daughter Elizabeth was taken under the protection of Lady Davenant, a widow lady, by whom she was recommended to Sir William Davenant, the patentee of the theatre in Lincoln's-inn-fields: her first efforts were unsuccessful; but afterwards, by the instructions of the celebrated Earl of Rochester, she became the most eminent actress that the stage had then

seen. She first distinguished herself by acting Isabella, in the tragedy of Mustapha, and was thought to excel very much in personating Queen Elizabeth, and in the character of Roxana. Mrs. Barry's last appearance was April 8, 1709, when she acted in the play of Love for Love (which was performed for Betterton's benefit) and spoke the epilogue. This was three years after she had retired from the stage. The following inscription is on a marble tablet affixed to a pillar between the south aisle and the nave of Acton church. "Near this place lies the body of Elizabeth Barry, of the parish of St. Mary, Savoy, who departed this life the 7th of November 1713. Aged 55 years."[1]

The entry in the original parish register reads *"Mrs. Eliz: Barry was Buryed in the Pish Church of Acton in the South oyle under ye End of Madam Lambe Pew being att ye uper End between ye two Pillers she was Buryed the 12th day of Novmber 1713".*

My research has now revealed, I believe for the first time, the identity of 'Madam Lambe', whose forename was Anne. She was the wife of Henry Lambe, Citizen and Goldsmith of London, and both resided at Acton. The following indenture, dated 1717, regarding their residence of the Mansion House which was known by the name of Fosters at East Acton, was made when Anne Lambe had been a widow for five years. Henry, her husband, had been buried on the 9th day of July 1712 at St. Mary's Church,

---

[1] Daniel Lysons, 'Acton', in *The Environs of London: Volume 2, County of Middlesex* (London, 1795), pp. 1-20. *British History Online* http://www.british-history.ac.uk/london-environs/vol2/pp1-20

MRS ELIZABETH BARRY (1658-1713)

Acton, and his will was proved on the 4th of August following. The Indenture assigned the property to a Thomas Hamilton Esq. of St. James's, Westminster:

APPENDIX II.

LEASE OF FEBRUARY 3rd, 1717, DESCRIBING THE PROPERTY.

Lamb and Hamilton

This Indenture having date 3rd of Feby 1717 made between Ann Lamb, Widow, Executrix and residuary legatee of Henry Lamb, Citizen and Goldsmith of London, deceased, and Thomas Hamilton, of the Parish of St. James, Westminster, Esqre., in the County of Middx., remembering that by an Indenture tripartite dated the second day of May 1686 between the Wardens and Commonalty of the Mistry of Goldsmiths of the City of London of the first part Thomas Fowles, Esqre, one of the Aldermen of the City of London, Richard Moore, John Coggs, Richard Hoare, Peter Floyer, and Richard Lascelles, Citizens and Goldsmiths of London, customary tenants of the Manor of Acton in the County of Middlesex of the second part and Henry Lamb Citizen and Goldsmith of the City of London, of the third part the said Wardens and Commonalty of the Mistry of the Goldsmiths in pursuance of certain articles of agreement made the 26th day of January preceding the date of the said Indenture and made between the said Wardens and

Commonalty of the Mistry of Goldsmiths of the one part and the said Henry Lamb of the other part and for and consideration therein mentioned did demise lett and to farm lett unto the said Henry Lamb all and singular their freehold messuages, lands tenements and hereditaments whatever of the said Wardens and Commonalty of the Mistry of Goldsmiths situate, lyeing and being in Acton in the County of Middlesex then or late in the occupation of Thomas Brumley, Edmond Riddle, William Pilsburgh, Robert Pratt, and Thos. Knowles, all which said freehold premises were by John Peryn Esqre by his last will and testament devised to the said Wardens and Commonalty of the Mistry of Goldsmiths and their successors, and also did demise, lett, and to farm lett to the said Henry Lamb all that their Capitall Messuage or Mansion House with all barns stables and outhouses thereunto adjoining together with all yards backsides orchards profits and commodities thereunto belonging situate and being in East Acton aforesaid usually called or known by the name of Fosters or by what other name or names soever the same is called or known also 5 crofts of land and 57½ acres of arable land and meadow or pasture ground . . . . and likewise all that other piece of ground in East Acton abovesaid lying near the aforesaid mansion house called Fosters and likewise one messuage or tenement with all barns, stables, etc., with all their seven closes of arable land meadow and pasture and woods and likewise 4

MRS ELIZABETH BARRY (1658-1713)

parcells of land containing by estimation 20½ acres of land be it more or less and all their two crofts late or sometime one croft in East Acton aforesaid, and likewise half an acre of land there upon which one tenement or cottage with a barn and other outhouses was built and also all that their one tenement or cottage . . . . and likewise two acres of arable land known by the name of Curleats Curlewyns and also 24 perches of land in length being long since used as a way within the Mannor of Acton aforesaid and also one messuage or tenement with all barns, etc., and likewise divers pieces or parcells of land meadows pastures and feedings containing in all 30 acres by estimation be it more or less pertaining to the said messuage or tenement and also one half acre of arable land lyeing in Eastfield in the Parish of Acton abutting on the land formerly of one Sir Richd Ashfield on the South and West, on the land formerly belonging to one Nicholas Vincent towards the North and upon the Warple towards the East, and likewise one acre of land lyeing in the same field abutting upon the lands formerly of the said Sir Richd Ashfield towards the South and West the land formerly of one James Cookson towards the North and on the Warple towards the East and likewise one other acre of land lyeing in the same field abutting upon the land formerly of the said Sir Richard Ashfeild towards the West and North on the lands formerly belonging to the said James Cookson towards the South and upon the Warple towards the East and also two parcells of customary lands lying and being in the Eastfield within the parish of Acton aforesaid one acre be it more or less abutts upon the land formerly belonging to the said Sir Richd Ashfield towards the North and West, upon the land heretofore belonging to one Andrew Wright towards the South and upon the Warple towards the East and the other parcell containing by estimation (measurement omitted) be it more or less as it is limitted and bounded upon the lands heretofore of the said Sir Richd Ashfield towards the West, the land heretofore of the said Andrew Wright towards the North, the land heretofore of the aforesaid James Cookson on the South and upon the Warple towards the East, which said last mentioned premises were copyhold of the Mannor of Acton and were devised by the said John Peryn by his last will for several uses and purposes therein mentioned to Thomas Smith, William Gibbons, William Harborow, John Gallibrand, Henry Pinckney, John Austin, Anthony Fficketts all since dead, and the said Richard Moore now surviving

. . . . etc., etc.,

The term was for the residue of 61 years and the rent £182.[2]

---

[2] Philip Norman, 'Appendix 2: Lease of 1717', in *Survey of London Monograph 7, East Acton Manor House* (London, 1921), pp. 26-27. British History Online
http://www.british-history.ac.uk/survey-london/bk7/pp26-27

MRS ELIZABETH BARRY (1658-1713)

Mrs. Anne Lambe made her last will and testament on the 7th of May 1727 whilst still residing in East Acton, and on her death she was interred, on the 3rd of August 1728, at the church at Acton, in the vault beside her late husband.

The Lambes' manor house, which had probably been rebuilt after 1686 by Henry Lambe when he became its lessee was, sadly, demolished in 1911.

There was also an incident in 1693, regarding Henry, when he was attacked upon the road when driving to his house at Acton:

> Nicholas Charleton. Breaking Peace: wounding. 26th April 1693 Reference Number: t16930426-56. Verdict: Not Guilty.
>
> These men were sworn to Try Mr. Nicholas Charleton.
>
> John Kene.
> Matthew Bateman.
> Timothy Thornbury.
> Richard Bealing.
> Edward Fuller.
> Symon Smith.
> William Thornbury.
> Joseph Blisset.
> Henry Russel.
> Henry Jones.
> William Willis.
> William Thompson.
>
> Nicholas Charleton, who was tried the last Sessions for stopping Mr. Henry Lamb, Gent. as

he was riding in his Coach to his House near Acton, in Company of four men more, supposed to be High-way men, was now again tried upon Coventry's Act, for malicious Maiming of him, with an intent to disfigure him; Mr. Lamb said, that five of them came up to his Coach, swearing great Oaths, shooting off no less than nine Pistols against him, one of which shot his Watch; which was in his Fob-pocket, and did him no harm; another shot him upon the Middle-finger of his Right-hand, and almost broke it in pieces; but Mr. Lamb only saw the Prisoner's Face by the flashing of the Powder; and there were others who said they met the Prisoner upon the Road the same day; Mr. Lamb shot one Keeling Baford dead upon the spot, and wounded another before they went off: The Prisoner produced several Witness to prove that he was all that day at Greenwich, particularly the two Watermen, who took him up at Westminster about 8 o Clock in the Morning, and brought him home about 7 or 8 at Night; there were others that saw him there, which they were very sure of, by reason that the Lords of the Admiralty dined there the same day, which was the 21st of January last; So after the Jury had consider'd a considerable time, they brought him in not guilty.[3]

According to bookseller and publisher Edmund Curll (*c.1675-1747)*, in his biography of Elizabeth Barry, her

---

3   *Old Bailey Proceedings Online* (www.oldbaileyonline.org,), April 1693, trial of Nicholas Charleton (t16930426-56).

MRS ELIZABETH BARRY (1658-1713)

father was a *gentleman of an ancient family and good estate,* a Mr. Robert Barry, Barrister at Law, later known as Colonel Barry through his raising of arms for Charles I during the English Civil Wars. This generous act apparently depleted his estate and as such made difficulties for his family. In other accounts her father is named as Edward Barry, so there is immediate confusion as to who Elizabeth's father really was. In *The history of the English stage, from the restoration to the present time. Including the lives, characters and amours, of the most eminent actors and actresses. With instructions for public speaking; wherein the action and utterance of the bar, stage, and pulpit are distinctly considered* by Thomas Betterton *(c.1635-1710),* believed to have been in collaboration with Edmund Curll *(1675-1747)* and published in 1741, there are, on page thirteen, chapter two, *Memoirs of Mrs. Barry,* beginning with:

> *Elizabeth Barry* was the Daughter of *Robert Barry*, Esq; Barrister at Law; a Gentleman of an ancient Family, and good Estate.
> At the Beginning of the Civil Wars, when King *Charles* invited all his Loyal Subjects to take up Arms in his Defence, Mr. *Barry* raised a Regiment for his Majesty's Service, composed of his Neighbours and Tenants, equipping and maintaining them a considerable Time at his own Expence. This as it ever after, made him known by the Title of Colonel *Barry*, it also so far incumbered his Estate, as to oblige his Children, when grown up, to make their own Fortunes in the World.

Musings on Mrs. Elizabeth Barry and Her Friends

The Lady *D'Avenant*, who had been several Years a Widow, and a particular Friend of Sir *William D'Avenant*, having the greatest Friendship for Col. *Barry*, took his Daughter, when young, and gave her a good Education. Lady *D' Avenant* made her not only her Companion, but carried her wherever she visited. Mrs. *Barry* by frequently conversing with Ladies of the first Rank and best Sense, became soon Mistress of that Behaviour which sets off the well-bred Gentlewoman.

Considering this was published some twenty-eight years after the death of Elizabeth Barry, in 1713, one does feel a little unsure of its reliability as to the parentage of the actress. Edmund Curll was apparently notorious for publishing biographies of famous people which included inaccuracies and inventions. Was this the case in Elizabeth's biography? Twenty-eight years is a long time to remember accurate details of someone's life, unless of course contemporary notes had been made by the author, which is very doubtful. There have been no references regarding the identity of Mrs. Barry's father other than to those of a Robert or an Edward noted above. The *Robert Barry* account has been accepted universally as the truth. However, with research, there has not been found, so far, anyone who would truly fit the bill of either a Robert or an Edward Barry, Barrister at Law and Royalist Colonel...intriguing.

The following is a transcription of Mrs. Barry's will, showing who were her legatees receiving money, real and personal estate, and the Newbury mills:

MRS ELIZABETH BARRY (1658-1713)

In the Name of God Amen I Elizabeth Barry Spinster being sick in body but of sound mind and memory praised be God for the same doe make and ordaine this my last will and Testament Imprimis I committ my Soul into the hands of Almighty God and my Body to the Earth to be decently buried and as for my estate I give and dispose as follows Item I give to Mr Gabriel Ballam Gent my Estate at Newbury consisting of mills. I give to Mrs Cary Twenty pounds. I give to Mrs Bracegirdle and Mrs Phubs Twenty pounds each Item I will that Two hundred pounds shall be to save Mrs Bracegirdle harmless from any Debt of the Play-House Item I give to Mrs Hawker wife of Thomas Hawker Painter Twenty pounds Item I give the residue and remainder of my whole Estate whatsoever both Reall and personall (after my Debts paid) to John Custis Gent formerly Page to the Prince and Abigal Stackhouse Spinster whom I make Executors of this my last Will to be divided equally between them Hereby Revoking all former wills by me made In wittness whereof I have hereunto sett my hand and seal this fourth day of November Anno Dmi. One thousand seven hundred and Thirteen. E. Barry. Signed Sealed Published and Declared to be the last Will and Testament of Eliz: Barry in the presence of Anne Hodge, the mark of Katherine Miller. Rich: Barrow[4]

---

4 Will of Elizabeth Barry, Spinster. The National Archives. PROB 11/536/276.

Musings on Mrs. Elizabeth Barry and Her Friends

Also attached to her will is the following, which surprisingly occurred some thirty-four years after her death:

> On the first day of March in the year of our Lord 1747 administration (with the will annexed) of the goods chattles and credits of Elizabeth Barry late of the parish of St. Mary le Savoy in the county of Middlesex spinster deceased left unadministered by John Custis and Abigail Overton formerly Stackhouse (wife of Philip Overton) the Executors and residuary Legatees named in the said Will now also respectively deceased was granted to Mary Sayer formerly Overton (wife of James Sayer) the Administratrix of the Goods of the said Abigail Overton formerly Stackhouse deceased whilst living the surviving Executrix and residuary legatee named in the said will being first sworn duly to administer.[5]

Mary Sayer, formerly Overton, formerly Baker, married Philip Overton on the 4th of December 1734 at St. Dunstan in the West, Middlesex. Philip would have been fifty-three at the time of their marriage.

Mrs. Barry, the doyen of the London Stage met her end in the most tragic of circumstances.

> 'An actress, who was in London when Mrs Barry died, assured me, many years since that

---

5 Will of Elizabeth Barry, Spinster. The National Archives. PROB 11/536/276.

MRS ELIZABETH BARRY (1658-1713)

her death was owing to the bite of a favourite lap-dog, who, unknown to her, had been seized with madness'.[6]

Poor Elizabeth must have died in much pain, fever and delirium. However, during the horrors of her distemper and knowing for sure her death was imminent, she had wit enough to make a will and bequeath her wealth. Without any known family, Barry's close and varied friends were her chosen beneficiaries.

A chance discovery. As can be seen, one of the witnesses to Barry's will was *Rich: Barrow* (Richard Barrow). He also witnessed Mrs. Barry's lease of the Newbury Mills, dated 1706, so he appears to have been a close friend of Elizabeth's for several years. Richard Barrow, formerly gentleman of Hereford, but later of London made a will in 1723 and in it he states:

> ...*whereas I have had severall dealings and Transactions with my most worthy Lady and Mistress the right Honourable Elizabeth Countess of Sandwich and for the preventing all manner of difference and disputes with a Lady from whom I have had so many Obligations I will that my Executor hereafter named Shall give her a general Discharge upon Condition that she likewise does the same but I hope that when it may be a Convenient time that she will pay at such payment as she pleases to my Sister Elizabeth Murphy the two hundred pounds that*

---

6   Dramatic Miscellanies, Volume III. Thomas Davies. pp 121-122. 1784

Musings on Mrs. Elizabeth Barry and Her Friends

M'' Baron Page was to have paid me Item I will that my Executor do deliver unto the said Countess all her Boxes and Cases that are in my Lodgings...

Richard's lodgings were in King Street, St. James's, London.

The Right Honourable Elizabeth Countess of Sandwich *(1674-1757)* was one of the daughters of John Wilmot, 2nd Earl of Rochester *(1647-1680)*, Elizabeth Barry's one time lover. At the time of Richard's will, in 1723, Countess Sandwich was forty-nine years old. She had been, it appears, unhappily married for some time, seemingly due to her husband, Edward Montagu, 3rd Earl of Sandwich's purported insanity; he died in 1729 at the age of fifty-nine. The Earl had wed Elizabeth in 1689 and they had two children; a daughter Elizabeth who died in infancy and a son Edward Richard Montagu, Viscount Hinchingbrooke, born in 1692, who died at the young age of thirty in 1722. Might the Countess's hapless marriage have brought a particular closeness with the widowed Richard Barrow?

And a further interesting discovery in the will: *"Item I desire the honour of her Grace the Duchess of Hamilton to accept of Mrs Barrys picture which my Executor will waite on her Grace with"*. This Duchess of Hamilton was Lady Anne Cochrane *(1707-1724)* the daughter of John Cochrane, 4th Earl of Dundonald *(1686-1720)* and his wife Anne Murray *(1697-1710)*. Anne Cochrane was the first wife of James Hamilton, 5th Duke of Hamilton *(1703-1743)* and was only six years old at the time of Barry's death. The 5th Duke was the son of James Hamilton, 4th Duke of Hamilton and 1st Duke of Brandon KG KT *(1658-1712)*, he of the famous duel with Charles Mohun, 4th Baron Mohun

MRS ELIZABETH BARRY (1658-1713)

(c.1675-1712) over a disputed inheritance. The duel took place in Hyde Park, London, on the 15th of November 1712, wherein both men were mortally wounded. Was this picture, then in the possession of Barrow, the original by Sir Godfrey Kneller? Or is there another portrait of Barry that has yet to come to light?

Sadly, Anne died from childbirth of her only child, James George Hamilton, later 6th Duke of Hamilton and 3rd Duke of Brandon, KT *(1724-1758)*, when she was just seventeen years old. At the time of Richard Barrow's will, made in December 1723, Anne was no doubt healthy and had just become pregnant, only to die eight months later. The generous gift of Elizabeth Barry's picture was tragically not enjoyed by her for very long.

Richard Barrow was the son of Richard and Martha Barrow who were married on the 10th of February 1669 at St. Sepulchre, Holborn, London. Richard was christened at St. Bride's, Fleet Street, London on the 25th of June 1674. His two surviving sisters, Martha who married an Edmund Loyd Esq., and an Elizabeth Murphy, wife of Dr. [John] Murphy, are named in his will. His other siblings, Ursula, Anne, Mary, Margaret and brother James had all predeceased him.

Transcription of Richard Barrow's will:

> **In the Name of God Amen** I Richard Barrow of Bullingham of the County of Hereford Gentleman and now resideing in King Street St. James's being weak in body but of sound mind and memory do make and ordaine this my last will and Testament revoking all other wills by me formerly made Imprimis I Recommend my

soul into the hands of God who gave it my body to be buried in the most private manner as near the body of my dear Wife in St. James's Vault as may be and as for my reall and personall Estate I dispose of in manner and form following whereas I stand possessed of two Thousand pounds Stock in the Bank of England and two Thousand pounds in the Mission Bank the Stock in the said two Companys was only transferred to me for the payment of three hundred per annum during my naturall life now I will that my Executor hereafter named shall after my decease transferr unto Mr Lateward Executor or Administrator to M^r. Meriweather all the said Stock upon the payment of what Arrears shall be due to me the day of my decease and whereas I have had severall dealings and Transactions with my most worthy Lady and Mistress the right Honourable Elizabeth Countess of Sandwich and for the preventing all manner of difference and disputes with a Lady from whom I have had so many Obligations I will that my Executor hereafter named Shall give her a general Discharge upon Condition that she likewise does the same but I hope that when it may be a Convenient time that she will pay at such payment as she pleases to my Sister Elizabeth Murphy the two hundred pounds that Mr Baron Page was to have paid me Item I will that my Executor do deliver unto the said Countess all her Boxes and Cases that are in my Lodgings Item I will that my Executor give to my old Acquaintance and Frien Sir Jacob Banks a

MRS ELIZABETH BARRY (1658-1713)

Generall Discharge and also a Discharge for the money due to my Aunt Church to whom I am Executor which sume was secured by a Judgement he giving a Release to my Executor and whereas there is a small sume of money due to me from William Phillips Esquire if he pleases to accept a Release from my Executor I Appoint him to give one and deliver up his Note And the like Release to my good Friend Captain Thomas Hamilton of a debt due from him to me Item I will that my Executor give a Generall Release to M^r. Hollaway he doing the same to my Executor and also I give him the sume of twenty pounds but not for mourning and whereas I am obliged to pay to my Sister Martha Loyd free and Exclusive from her Husband the Interest of the sume of Six hundred pounds pursuant to the Will of my Aunt Church deceased during her life and afterwards to her two Daughters share and share alike which money I have in my hands pursuant to the said Will I do direct my Executor to pay to my said Sister the Interest as it shall become due and the said principall to the said Daughters after her decease and I do hereby charge my reall Estate with the payment thereof Item I give and devise to my said Sister Elizabeth Murphy the sume of Fifty pounds per Annum during her life free from all Taxes or payments whatsoever by quarterly payments the first quarterly payment to commence from my death and I will that my Heir and Executor hereafter named shall only pay the same into her own hands free and exclusive from her present or any other after Husband and what with this Fifty pounds per Annum and thirty pounds that was formerly charged upon my estate amounts to the sume of four score pounds a year which shall allways stand charged upon my Reall Estate shall the determination of the same by the death of my same Sister which payments from time to time shall be legally discharged by her own receipt Item I give to my said Sister Murphy to be paid into her own hands the sume of Fifty pounds Item I confirm the bond which I formerly gave to Mrs Elizabeth Brownsworth for three hundred pounds Item I give to her her own picture and my Lady Banbury's and Ten Guineas but not for mourning and the like sume of ten Guineas to her Mother and whereas I stand indebted to D^{r}. Murphy by Note in the sume of One hundred pounds there being an Agreement that if he did let the money remain in my hands I was to give him two hundred pounds which he having performed I will that my Executor pay him or his Order on the delivery of my Note of one hundred pounds with ten pounds indorsed upon it the sume of two hundred pounds in full satisfaction of the said note Item I give to my neice Martha Loyd the sume of one hundred pounds to be paid into her own hands exclusive from her Husband which receipt of my said Sister shall be a discharge to my Executor Item I give to my Nephew John Loyd the sume of one hundred pounds and after the decease of my sister Elizabeth Murphy I give him the further

MRS ELIZABETH BARRY (1658-1713)

sume of three hundred pounds Item I give to my Nephew Richard Loyd and my Neice Elizabeth Loyd the sume of one hundred pounds each to be paid them at the age of twenty two years with Interest till the said sumes becomes payable Item I give to my Cozen Elizabeth Read the sum of Fifty pounds Item I give to my Father and my Old Servant Thomas Merrick of Bullingham fifty pounds Item I give to the poor of the parish of Bullingham Twenty pounds Item I desire the Honour of her Grace the Duchess of Hamilton to accept of Mrs Barrys picture which my Executor will waite on her Grace with Item I give to my Maid Mary the sum of twenty pounds and a quarters wages and board wages Item I give to my Man Edmund Cally the sume of ten pounds and a quarters wages and board wages and all my wearing Cloaths both woollen and linnen to be equally divided between my said two servants. Item I give to my Sister Murphy the intire furniture that properly belongs to my bed Chamber and the linnen in the Chest and also Six Silver hafted Knives Six Silver spoons and Six Silver forkes all which she is to take her choice of and whereas I stand seized and possessed of a reall Estate called the manor of Bullingham in the County of Hereford and other Lands in the said County now I do hereby give and devise all my said Lands Tenements and hereditaments whatsoever lying and being in the said County of Hereford to my loving Friend and Cozen John Skinner of Charles Street Westminster to hold to him and his Heirs for

Musings on Mrs. Elizabeth Barry and Her Friends

ever Upon this Speciall Trust and confidence that he his Heirs Executors or Administrators shall by sale mortgage or otherwise raise money from time to time as he or they shall think fit to pay all my debts Legacys and Funerall Expenses and the overplus to him and his heirs Item I give to my said Couzen Skinner all my personall estate whatsoever and I do hereby Constitute and Appoint him the said John Skinner Sole Executor of this my last will and Testament in Witness whereof I the said Richard Barrow have to this my last will and Testament containing two sheets of paper to the first whereof set my hand and to this last my hand and seale this Eighth day of December in the Tenth year of the Reigne of our Soveraigne Lord George by the Grace of God of Great Britain France and Ireland King Defender of the Faith Anno Domini 1723 Rich Barrow Signed Sealed published and declared by the said Richard Barrow being two sheets of paper as and for his last will and Testament in the presence of us who have subscribed our names at witnesses hereto in his presence the words (and his Heirs being interlined) Peregrina Sissor Giles Penne J Bucknastow[7]

Aunt Church was Ursula Church, sister of Martha, Richard's mother. The address in the aunt's will dated 1716 is situate in the parish of St. Paul, Covent Garden,

---

[7] Will of Richard Barrow, Gentleman of King Street Saint James, Middlesex. Reference: PROB 11/594/414. The National Archives.

MRS ELIZABETH BARRY (1658-1713)

Middlesex, the same residence as Martha. Ursula more than likely lived with her sister after she was widowed.

At the close of 1723, tragedy struck the Barrow family. Soon after making his will on the 8th of December, Richard Barrow died, his probate being dated the 30th of December. His mother too had made her will, on the 23rd of July that year, and she died within five months, her probate being dated the 10th of December the same year.

Coincidently, a very famous London citizen died just two months after Richard; the brilliant Sir Christopher Wren, who lived to the great age of ninety-one years. Richard's residence was in King Street, St. James's, whilst Wren's London residence was nearby on St. James's Street, so they were near neighbours, and might have known each other by acquaintance.

There is also to be found an Elizabeth Barry living in Bury Street, St. James's, in the year 1700. As King Street abuts Bury Street, surely it is not just a coincidence that an Elizabeth Barry and Richard Barrow lived so near to each other?

Richard's friends were very varied indeed and included some Jacobite sympathizers also named in his will. One such was supposed Jacobite, Jacob Banks (Bancks) *(1662-1724)* of Milton Abbas, Dorset and of Somerford, Hants. He was a Swedish naval officer in the British service, and became a Tory Member of Parliament, representing Minehead in 1698. He was an old friend and acquaintance of Richard Barrow and in his will gives Banks a general discharge of any money due. Banks was implicated in the *Gyllenberg Plot*, a Jacobite conspiracy in 1716/17, and duly taken into custody with another accused conspirator, Charles Caesar *(1673-1741)*. Caesar was Treasurer of the Navy from 1711 to 1714. Banks was released on bail of

Musings on Mrs. Elizabeth Barry and Her Friends

£5,000 after the authorities failed to find any proof of his guilt. This all begs the question, was Richard Barrow a Jacobite? His *Lady and Mistress,* the Right Honourable Elizabeth Countess of Sandwich *(1674-1757)* certainly was.[8] She abandoned England for France after the death of her husband in 1729, she having visited the country previously in the late 1690s.

Letters between Charles Saint-Évremond *(1613-1703)* and Ninon de l'Enclos *(1620-1705),* who were two close friends of the Countess, show how much she was widely loved and admired by all who met her in the salons of aristocratic Parisians and likewise by many of England's elite.

Richard Barrow's brother-in-law, Dr. John Murphy, apparently too was a Jacobite and was a participating rebel in the unsuccessful Jacobite rising of 1715. He was instrumental in introducing Sergeant Stephen Lynch, an Irishman born in Flanders and also a participant in the 1715 rising, to fellow conspirator and Middle Temple lawyer Christopher Layer *(1683-1723),* in connection with the Atterbury Plot of 1722. This Jacobite plot was led by Francis Atterbury *(1663-1732),* Bishop of Rochester and Dean of Westminster. Both Lynch and Layer were arrested, but Lynch turned evidence whilst Layer was tried for treason, the case beginning on the 31st of October 1722. Found guilty, Layer suffered the barbarous fate of many traitors and was hanged, drawn and quartered at Tyburn on the 17th of May 1723.

---

8   Elizabeth Montagu Countess of Sandwich (1674-1757): lord Rochester's Jacobite daughter who abandoned England for France. Susan Margaret Cooper. 2018.
https://www.amazon.co.uk/dp/B07DH9BDSG/ref=sr_1_1?s=digital-text&ie=UTF8&qid=1528095771&sr=1-1&keywords=Elizabeth+Montagu

MRS ELIZABETH BARRY (1658-1713)

By contrast, Mr. Baron Page mentioned in the will, was a man of the law and often sat as a Judge in Court proceedings. However, there is no evidence he held Jacobite sympathies.

Old Bailey Proceedings

4th December 1723

THE PROCEEDINGS ON THE KING's Commission of the Peace, AND Oyer and Terminer, and Goal-Delivery of Newgate, held for the CITY of London and COUNTY of Middlesex, at Justice Hall in the Old Bailey,

On Wednesday, Thursday, Friday, Saturday, and Thursday, being the 4th, 5th, 6th, 7th, and 12th of December, in the Tenth Year of His MAJESTY's Reign,

BEFORE the Right Honourable Sir PETER DELME, Kt. Lord Mayor of the City of London; the Lord chief Justice King, Mr. Baron Page, John Raby, Esq; Deputy Recorder; and several of His Majesty's Justices of the Peace for the City of London and Country of Middlesex.[9]

Mrs. Elizabeth Brownsworth, named in the will, was the daughter of Hannah Brownsworth (née Price) who was sister to Elizabeth, Lady Banbury. Hannah's house was in St. James's Street, London, very near to where Richard

---

9 *Old Bailey Proceedings Online* (www.oldbaileyonline.org,version 8.0,), December 1723 (17231204).

Musings on Mrs. Elizabeth Barry and Her Friends

lived, and he must have been a very great friend of these women, having in his possession pictures of both Elizabeth Brownsworth and of her aunt, Lady Banbury. One could assume by his owning Banbury's picture that he acknowledged her as the true Countess of Banbury.

This Lady Banbury was formerly an actress for a short time before she married Charles Knollys, 4th Earl of Banbury *(1662-1740)* in Verona, Italy on the 7th of April 1692. The marriage was not altogether a simple one, as Banbury had reportedly been married previously, on the 16th of May 1689, to Elizabeth Lister *(1663-1699)*, at the Nag's Head Coffee House, James Street, Covent Garden, whereby she took the title of Countess Banbury. The bride was the daughter of a Michael Lister of South Carlton, Lincolnshire and his wife, Ann. A Court case instigated by Elizabeth Price ensued, it being dismissed by the Court of Delegates in 1697. The Court claimed that Elizabeth Lister was the true Countess of Banbury, owing to her being of good reputation (not an actress?) and the mother of Earl Banbury's children. They say 'All's fair in love and war', but I think not in this case.[10]

Elizabeth Brownsworth seems to have had a more traditional and settled life than her aunt. This Elizabeth, a spinster of twenty-five, married a lawyer, Gibbons Bagnal, gentleman and widower of the Inner Temple, aged then above forty, at St. Stephen, Coleman Street, London, on the 16th of November 1732. When Elizabeth married him he had four offspring living, namely: Ann Bagnal; a son Gibbons Bagnal; Mary Bagnal and Sarah Bagnal. Elizabeth died a widow in 1758, her husband predeceasing her by

---

10 The True Countess of Banbury's Case Relating to Her Marriage Rightly Stated in a Letter to the Lord Banbury. London. Printed n the Year MDCXCVI

MRS ELIZABETH BARRY (1658-1713)

fifteen years. At the time Elizabeth made her will, she was living in Downing Street, Westminster and seemed to be a lady of some wealth, with two leased properties; one in Queen Square in the parish of St. George the Martyr and the other in New Windsor in the county of Berkshire. All her step-children at the time she made her will benefited from her real and personal estate, with the exception of the son, then Reverend Gibbons, whose own children received like shares.

And it appears that things did not go altogether smoothly with regard to Richard Barrow's family, four years after his death, as this 1727 Court of Chancery case reveals. Held at The National Archives, Kew, Reference C 11/2412/17. Short Title: Skinner. v. Lloyd. Plaintiffs: John Skinner, gent of Westminster, Middlesex. Defendants: Edmund Lloyd, Esq. and Martha Lloyd his wife, Dr. John Murphy and Elizabeth Murphy his wife. Skinner was the sole executor of Richard's will and legatee of his personal estate and of his lands, tenements and hereditaments whatsoever lying and being in the said county of Hereford. No doubt there was some disagreement as to money, as is often the case with family disputes.

***

It is quite revealing that at the end of her life Elizabeth Barry had very few real close friends, as her will proves. There are only two men mentioned in the will; Gabriel Ballam and John Custis. Ballam was unmarried but Custis had a wife and daughter. Therefore Ballam seemed to be the only man then in her life probably as both friend and

Musings on Mrs. Elizabeth Barry and Her Friends

lover. One can assume that many of her past lovers, excluding the Earl of Rochester of course, were long forgotten and more than likely these relationships were not some of the most memorable episodes in her life. All the others named in the will are women; Mrs. Cary, Mrs. Bracegirdle, Mrs. Phubs, Mrs. Hawker and Abigal Stackhouse. Who Mrs. Cary and Mrs. Phubs were is a mystery. Probably they were live-in companions or servants to Mrs. Barry. Whatever the truth, she obviously was very fond of them, bequeathing them a tidy sum of twenty pounds each, today's equivalent of approximately two thousand pounds, with the painter's wife, Mrs. Hawker, receiving the same amount. It is believed that at the time of Elizabeth's will Mrs. Hawker's husband would have still been alive, but probably not a wealthy man, even after he moved to No. 10-11 Great Piazza living there between 1682-1685, hoping to gain greatly from that previous occupants address, that of the famous portrait painter, Sir Peter Lely *(1618-1680)*. However, it is generally believed that Court painter, Thomas Hawker was buried at Covent Garden, on the 5th day of November 1699, but research has revealed that *this* burial was of a child *Thomas son of Peter Hawker.* A date of c.1722 is also suggested to be the date of the painter's demise and this would seem to be more feasible.

As for the celebrated actress Anne Bracegirdle *(1671-1748),* who had been a fellow actress and friend of Mrs. Barry for many years, she received from the will the vast sum of two hundred pounds, today's equivalent of some twenty thousand pounds! That sum would certainly have kept her *harmless from any debt of the Play-House.*

The two residuary legatees, John Custis and Abigal Stackhouse, would appear to be unconnected to each other,

MRS ELIZABETH BARRY (1658-1713)

however research *has* revealed a connection here. Although Abigal was a spinster at the time of Mrs. Barry's death, she did however later marry Philip Overton *(c.1681-1745)* Stationer of London, in 1714. Overton was a well-known print publisher, a business he established in Fleet Street, London c.1707. Surprisingly, Philip did have a connection with John Custis, whose first wife was a Mary. John and Mary had a daughter Henrietta Maria Custis, baptized 1684 at St. Dunstan in the West, when her family were living in Whitefriars. Henrietta never married, but in her will she leaves to her cousin Philip Overton the sum of twenty pounds. Therefore Mary Custis must have been a kinswoman of Overton and possibly a friend of Abigal, and might have introduced Philip to her. Henrietta is mentioned in her father's will along with his second wife, Elizabeth, who in *her* will dated 1715, when she had been widowed, refers to Henrietta as *my loving daughter in law* (step-daughter). Elizabeth died shortly after making her will.

Philip Overton died in 1744, his will proved that year. Later, on the 6th January 1746/7, Mary Overton, widow, married James Sayer at Christ Church, Spitalfields, she tragically dying in 1748 after the birth of their daughter Letitia. Her husband, James died forty-two years later at the age of eighty. Sayer was the brother of Robert Sayer *(1725-1797),* a leading publisher and seller of prints, maps and maritime charts.

John Custis, was Page of the Backstairs to Prince George of Denmark and Norway, Duke of Cumberland *(1653-1708)*, husband to Queen Anne *(1665-1714)*. In this role Custis was earning, in 1709, £80.00 per annum:

> *Pages of the Backstairs:* Peter Laroche (Page of the Backstairs and barber) 140*l.* per an.; Daniel

Musings on Mrs. Elizabeth Barry and Her Friends

Croharry 110*l*. per an.; Samuel Nash, John Custis each 80*l*. per an.[11]

And later, in 1714, Custis had been appointed Queen's waiter at the port of London with a salary of fifty-two pounds per annum.

There is an interesting letter, written by playwright and poet William Congreve *(1670-1729)*, referred to in *The Complete Works of William Congreve*, edited by Montague Summers. Vol. 1. The Nonesuch Press. 1923. p. 101, regarding a picture of the 2nd Earl of Rochester that was in the possession of Mrs. Barry. Although this letter is not dated it must have been written shortly after her death in 1713:

> S^r
> if you see M^r: Custis to night pray know of him if it be possible for me to have as picture of Ld Rochester which was Mrs. Barrys. I think it is a head. I think it is not as a painting any very great mater, however I have a very particular reason why. I would have it at any reasonable rate at least the refusal of it, if this can be don he will very much oblige his &
>   y^r:
>   very humble servant
> fryday even: Wm CONGREVE

---

11 'Warrant Books: August 1709, 1-10', in *Calendar of Treasury Books, Volume 23, 1709*, ed. William A Shaw (London, 1949), pp. 289-302. *British History Online* http://www.british-history.ac.uk/cal-treasury-books/vol23/pp289-302

MRS ELIZABETH BARRY (1658-1713)

It is obvious from this letter that John Custis must have been in possession of the picture among the items of real and personal estate divided equally between him and Abigal Stackhouse, it therefore being at his disposal. What a pity there was not an inventory of personal items listed with Mrs. Barry's will; that would possibly have shed some light on the Rochester painting referred to by Congreve of *not...any very great mater.*

Mrs. Barry's untimely death might have prompted John Custis into making his will on the 1st of March 1713, just four months after her demise:

> **In the Name of God Amen** I John Custis of the parish of Saint James's in the Liberty of Westminster in the County of Middlesex Gentleman being of sound and disposing mind memory and understanding do make this my Last Will and Testament in manner following Imprimis I give my soul into the Hands of Almighty God hoping for a joyfull Resurrection through the Merrits of Jesus Christ Item I give to my loving Wife Elizabeth Custis all and every part and parcel of my Plate Rings Jewels and Household Goods Household Stuff and Furniture of my House Item I give unto my Daughter Henrietta Maria Custis one Third part of all the rest and residue of my personal Estate the said residue into three parts being divided Item I give unto my said Wife Elizabeth the other two Third parts of the said residue of my personal Estate and I also give and bequeath unto her my said Wife the rest and residue of all my personal Estate whatsoever not herein before disposed of

Musings on Mrs. Elizabeth Barry and Her Friends

Item I give unto my Kinsman and freind M^r. Francis Hutchinson Ten Pounds to buy him mourning And lastly I make my said Wife sole Executrix of this my Last Will hereby revoking all and every former Wills and Will by me before made In Witness whereof I have hereunto sett my hand and seal this first day of March Anno Domini 1713 John Custis Signed Sealed Published and Declared by the said John Custis to be his Last Will and Testament in our presence who also then subscribed our names hereto in his presence. Tho: Jackson. John Rudge Cha Bainbridge.[12]

It seems that Rochester's portrait was not the only picture that Mrs. Barry had in her possession, she having at one time acquired the famous *Chandos Portrait of Shakespeare*. The picture, painted between 1600 and 1610, is attributed to artist John Taylor *(c.1585-1651)* and is named after the British peer and politician James Brydges, 3rd Duke of Chandos *(1731-1789)*, who formerly owned the painting. The picture is displayed in the National Portrait Gallery, London, it being given to the gallery at its foundation in 1856 by Francis Egerton, 1st Earl of Ellesmere *(1800-1857)*.

---

12 Will of John Custis, Gentleman of Saint James, Westminster, Middlesex.The National Archives. PROB 11/550/273.

MRS ELIZABETH BARRY (1658-1713)

William Shakespeare associated with John Taylor
oil on canvas, feigned oval, circa 1600-1610
Given by Francis Egerton, 1st Earl of Ellesmere, 1856
© National Portrait Gallery, London.

THE CHANDOS PORTRAIT OF SHAKSPEARE.

...The history of this very interesting portrait is shortly this. The Duke of Chandos obtained it by marriage with the daughter and heiress of a Mr. Nicholl, of Minchenden House, Southgate;

Mr. Nicholl obtained it from a Mr. Robert Keck, of the Inner Temple, — who gave (the first and best) Mrs. Barry, the actress, as Oldys tells us, forty guineas for it. Mrs. Barry had it from Betterton, — and Betterton had it from Sir William Davenant, who was a professed admirer of Shakspeare, and not unwilling to be thought his son. Davenant was born in 1605, and died in 1668; and Betterton (as every reader of Pepys will recollect) was the great actor belonging to the Duke's Theatre, of which Davenant was the patentee. The elder brother of Davenant (Parson Robert) had been heard to relate, as Aubrey informs us, that Shakspeare had often kissed Sir William when a boy.

Davenant lived quite near enough to Shakspeare's time to have obtained a genuine portrait of the poet whom he admired, — in an age, too, when the Shakspeare mania was not so strong as it is now. There is no doubt that this was the portrait which Davenant believed to be like Shakspeare; and which Kneller before 1692 copied and presented to glorious John Dryden,— who repaid the painter with one of the best of his admirable epistles.[13]

***

Mrs. Barry was the first to perform the role of Zara in Congreve's '*The Mourning Bride*', believed to have premiered in 1697 at the Lincoln's Inn Fields playhouse,

---
13 The Athenæum. Journal of English and Foreign Literature, Science, and the Fine Arts. London, Saturday, January, 1, 1848. p 397.

MRS ELIZABETH BARRY (1658-1713)

with Thomas Betterton in the play as Osmyn. The reason I mention this snippet is regarding Mrs. Barry's supposed ancestral roots *"of an ancient Family, and good Estate."* Whether true or not, there have been many undesirable comments and lampoons made about Mrs. Barry's supposed scandalous reputation, and no exception was the obscure mention (extract below) taken from *The Restoration Theatre* by Montague Summers, 1934, p.319, in an extremely lengthy poem *The Play-House. A Satyr* by Robert Gould 1685:

...When, let our Plays be acted half an Age,
W'ave but a third Days Gleaning of the Stage?
The rest is yours :— and hence your Sharers rise,
And once above us, all our Aid despise:
Hence has your *Osmin* drawn his Wealthy Lot,
And hence has *Zara* all her Thousands got:
Zara! That Proud, Opprobrious, Shameless Jilt,
Who like a Devil justifies her Guilt,
And feels no least Remorse for all the Blood sh'has spilt.
But prithee *Joe*, since so she boasts her Blood,
And few have yet her Lineage understood,
Tell me, in short, the Harlot's true Descent,
'Twill be a Favour that you shan't repent.

    Truly said *Joe*, as now the Matter goes,
What I shall speak must be beneath the Rose.
Her mother was a common Strumpet known,
Her Father half the Rabble of the Town.
Begot by Casual and Promiscous Lust,
She still retains the same Promiscuous Gust,
For Birth into a Suburb Cellar hurl'd,
The Strumpet came up Stairs into the World.

Musings on Mrs. Elizabeth Barry and Her Friends

At Twelve she'd freely in Coition join,
And far surpass'd the Honours of her Line.
As her Conception was a Complication,
So its Produce, alike, did serve the Nation;
Till by a Black, Successive Course of Ills,
She reach'd the Noble Post which now she fills;
Where, *Messalina* like, she treads the Stage,
And all Enjoys, but nothing can Asswage!...

It is not surprising that his violent attack on the theatre and its thespians, and particularly upon Mrs. Barry and Thomas Betterton, incensed these actors against Robert Gould *(c.1660-c.1709)*. They did their damnedest to prevent Gould's play *The Rival Sisters; or, The Violence of Love* from being accepted for production. Gould even had the weak excuse of saying ...*I put 'em in mind I was very Young when this Satyr was Written, and by Consequence cou'd not know the value of what I slighted.* Too late was the cry!

And a delightful few lines on Mrs. Barry in an anonymous poem *A Satire on the Players*:

...There's one, Heav'n bless us! by her cursed pride,
Thinks from the world her brutish lust to hide;
But will that pass in her, whose only sense,
Does lie in whoring, cheats, and impudence!
One that is pox all o'er, *Barry* her name,
That mercenary, prostituted dame;
Whose nauseous a----like *Tony's tap* does run:
Unpity'd fool, that can't her ulcer shun!
Tho' like a *Hackney* jade, just tir'd before,
And all her little fulsome stock run o're;
Tho' faces are distorted with mere pain,

MRS ELIZABETH BARRY (1658-1713)

So that wry mouth ne'er since came right again:
Yet ten times more she'd bear for slavish gain...[14]

However, the actor and dramatist Anthony Aston [performing name Mat Medley] *(c.1682-c.1753)* who knew Mrs. Barry depicted her in a slightly more favourable way; *She was not handsome, her Mouth opening most on the Right Side, which she strove to draw t'other Way, and at Times composing her Face as if sitting to have her Picture drawn. She was middle-siz'd, and had darkish Hair, light Eyes, dark Eyebrows, and was indifferently plump.* And Aston was also known to remark; *Mrs. Barry was woman to Lady Shelton of Norfolk (my godmother) when Lord Rochester took her on the stage, where for some time they could make nothing of her—she could neither sing nor dance, no, not in a country dance.*

The remarks of critic and playwright John Dennis *(1658-1734)* on Mrs. Barry were decidedly praising; *that incomparable Actress changing like Nature which she represents, from Passion to Passion, from Extream to Extream, with piercing Force and with easy Grace.*

And a glowing endorsement to the remarkable actress from Thomas Betterton, the leading actor of his day, *that she often so greatly exerted her art in an indifferent character, that her acting had given success to plays that would disgust the most patient reader.*

And long may Barry Live to Charm the Age. This wonderful sentiment on Mrs. Barry was expressed in The Epilogue, *Shakespeares Ghost,* spoken by John Baptista

---

14 The Posthumous Works of Mr. Samuel Butler, (Author of Hudibras). Written in the time of the Grand Rebellion, and in the reign of King Charles II. Being a collection of satire, speeches, and reflections upon those times. 3rd edition, London. M DCC XXX. pp 121-122.

Musings on Mrs. Elizabeth Barry and Her Friends

Verbruggen *(d.1708)*, in the play *Measure For Measure, or, Beauty The Best Advocate.* The drama, originally by William Shakespeare *(1564-1616)* had been much altered by Charles Gildon *(c.1665-1724).*

Enough your Cruelty Alive I knew;
And must I Dead be Persecuted too?
Injur'd so much of late upon the *Stage*,
My *Ghost* can bear no more; but comes to Rage.
My *Plays*, by *Scriblers,* Mangl'd I have seen;
By Lifeless *Actors* Murder'd on the *Scene*.
Fat *Falstaff* here, with Pleasure, I beheld,
Toss off his Bottle, and his *Truncheon* weild:
Such as I meant him, such the *Knight* appear'd;
He Bragg'd like *Falstaff*, and, like *Falstaff*, fear'd.
But when, on yonder *Stage*, the Knave was shewn
Ev'n by my Self, the Picture scarce was known.
Themselves, and not the Man I drew, they *Play'd*;
And Five *Dull Sots,* of One poor Coxcomb, made.
Hell! that on you such Tricks as these shou'd pass,
Or I be made the Burden of an *Ass!*
Oh! if *Machbeth*, or *Hamlet* ever pleas'd,
Or *Desdemona* e'r your Passions rais'd;
If *Brutus,* or the Bleeding *Caesar* e'r
Inspir'd your Pity, or provok'd your Fear,
Let me no more endure such Mighty VVrongs,
By *Scriblers* Folly, or by *Actors* Lungs.
So, late may *Betterton* for sake the *Stage*,
And long may *Barry* Live to Charm the *Age.*
May a New *Otway* Rise, and Learn to Move
The *Men* with *Terror*, and the *Fair* with *Love!*
Again, may *Congreve*, try the *Commic* Strain;
And *Wycherly* Revive his Ancient *Vein*:

MRS ELIZABETH BARRY (1658-1713)

Else may your Pleasure prove your greatest Curse;
And those who now *Write dully*, still *Write worse*.[15]

And still with Gildon:

> Gildon in his Comparison between the two Stages in 1702 makes Sullen say of Mrs. Barry— "What think you of the renowned Cleopatra?"
> *Critick*. By that nickname, so unfortunate to poor Antony, as the other has been to many an honest country Gentleman, I should guess whom you mean.
> *Sullen*. You take me right.
> *Critick*. In her time she has been the spirit of action everyway; nature made her for the delight of mankind; and till nature began to decay in her, all the town shared her bounty.
> *Ramble*. I do think that person the finest woman in the world upon the stage, and the ugliest woman off on't.
> *Sullen*. Age and intemperance are the fatal enemies of beauty; she's guilty of both; she has been a rioter in her time; but the edge of her appetite is long ago taken off; she still charms (as you say) upon the stage; and even off I don't think so rudely of her as you do: 'tis true, time

---

15 Measure for measure, or, Beauty the best advocate as it is acted at the theatre in Lincolns-Inn-Fields: written originally by Mr. Shakespear, and now very much alter'd, with additions of several entertainments of musick. https://quod.lib.umich.edu/e/eebo/A59508.0001.001/1:5?rgn=div1;view=fulltext

has turned up some of her furrows, but not to such a degree.

Ramble. To the degree of loathsomeness upon my faith; but on the stage, I am willing to let her still pass for an heroine.

Critick. And still off on't too, if all be true that is said of her.[16]

And a further piece adding to the credit of Mrs. Barry, when she played Princess Homais in The Royal Mischief (1696), a she-tragedy by Delarivier Manley *(c.1663-1724)*. The playwright had this to say:

> ...I do not doubt when the ladies have given themselves the trouble of reading and comparing it with others, they'll find the prejudice against our sex and not refuse me the satisfaction of entertaining them, nor themselves the pleasure of Mrs. Barry, who by all that saw her is concluded to have exceeded that perfection which before she was justly thought to have arrived at. My obligations to her were the greater, since against her own approbation, she excelled and made the part of an ill woman, not only entertaining, but admirable.[17]

To conclude on the good, the bad and the ugly of Mrs. Barry, for a typical Victorian view of her, English poet,

---

16 Some Account of the English Stage, from the Restoration in 1660 to 1830. Vol. II. Bath. 1832. pp 463-464
17 https://crrs.ca/new/wp-content/uploads/2012/11/OV17-Staging-Islam.pdf pp 46-46

MRS ELIZABETH BARRY (1658-1713)

author and critic, Sir Edmund William Gosse CB *(1849-1928)*, had this to say:

> Mrs. Barry was an ignoble, calculating woman; no generous act, even of frailty, is recorded of her. Whether or not, in rivalry with Mrs. Gwyn, she set her cap at royalty, she had a well-balanced sense of her own value, and smiled at nothing lower than an earl...[18]

My own views on Mrs. Barry are that she was no more mercenary than many of her contemporaries. I believe she was an educated, ambitious and witty woman who needed to survive as a single woman in a hostile mens' world. She worked hard for her gains, whether on stage or off it, and had many friends who respected her for who she was and who ignored her scurrilous male critics who were no doubt jealous of her fame and fortune. As for her affair with Rochester, this did not seem in any way to particularly tarnish her friendship with one of his daughters, Mallet Wilmot, Lady Lisburne *(1676-1709)* who married John Vaughan, 1st Viscount Lisburne *(1667-1721)*, as Mrs. Barry's rare letter proves.

And would Rochester's favourite niece, Anne Lee *(1659-1685)*, who was the first wife of nobleman and politician Thomas Wharton, 1st Marquess of Wharton *(1648-1715)*, leave a substantial sum to Mrs. Barry's young daughter *Elizabeth Barry* by Rochester if she had believed the scandalmongers. *little Barry*, as Honest John Cary Esq. *(c.1601-1702)*, Anne, Countess of Rochester's *(1614-1696)* faithful friend and steward, calls her in a letter dated 1685 to Edward Henry Lee, 1st Earl of Lichfield *(1663-1716)*,

---

18 Seventeenth-Century Studies. A contribution to The History of English Poetry. By Edmund W. Gosse. London. 1883. p. 278.

Musings on Mrs. Elizabeth Barry and Her Friends

died believed aged twelve. Sadly, she never gained that generous windfall that would have made her a very rich and highly sought after young lady:

> ...And upon this further Trust & confidence that they the said George Bradbury Francis Henry Carey & Thomas Baxter their Executors or Admin^{rs} by and out of the said Rents Issues & profitts or by Leases or Mortgages of any part or parts of the aforesaid Mannors Messuages Lands Tenements Hereditaments and p^{re}mises so before limitted to them for Five Hundred years do & shall raise advance and pay unto Elizabeth Barry naturall Daughter of John late Earle of Rochester if she shall happen to live to attaine to the age of One & Twenty years the full sum of Three thousand pounds of lawfull money of England...[19]

Whilst on the subject of little Barry, the following are my own thoughts as to the infant daughter *Elizabeth Clerke*, named in Rochester's will and who was to receive *Fourtie pounds Annuitie to commence from the day of my decease, and to continue during her life.* I have never truly believed that Elizabeth Clerke was their daughter, as there would be no logical reason whatsoever why she should have been called Clerke. Their daughter is quite clearly named Elizabeth Barry in the extract above. Perhaps Rochester had a further daughter by another mistress by the name of Clerke? It is noted that in a thesis of 1940 on Elizabeth

---

19 Indenture. Copy of Deed to lead uses of a fine dated 4th May 1685. A/CSC/1512. London Metropolitan Archives.

MRS ELIZABETH BARRY (1658-1713)

Barry there *is* mention that Rochester had a mistress by the name of Mrs. Clerke. Also Rochester had a menial servant by the name of William Clerke, a Scot and one time lawyer (not to be confused with William Clarke, an Englishman, also a lawyer and respected trustee of Rochester); was the infant Clerke a child of the Scot?

A letter dated the 23rd of November 1685, written five years after Rochester's will, adds weight to my suspicion. The letter from John Cary, addressed to the aforementioned Earl of Lichfield, is regarding family disputes involving property and legacies in connection with Thomas Wharton and his wife Anne. In it there is mentioned:

> ...*And all the Mannors & Lands therein particularly named in the County of Wilts. to her self for life and after that a lease of 500 years is made to Mr Bradbury my son Harry Cary & Mr Thomas Booker, for the raising & paying out of the rents & profits three thousand pounds to little Barry...*[20]

***

Elizabeth Barry died at Acton, West London, originally Middlesex, on the 7th of November 1713, four days after making her will and was buried in the church there, where there is a monument to her fixed high upon a wall inside.

There is also to be found a poignant poem to Elizabeth Barry, by one of the Harding brothers, either Silvester or Edward, in their publication of 1795 *The Biographical Mirrour,* in the chapter headed *Memoirs of Mrs. Barry*:

---

20 Oxfordshire History Centre. Collection reference: (E36/18/6/W/1). 6 051018

Musings on Mrs. Elizabeth Barry and Her Friends

To which the compiler of these anecdotes takes the liberty to subjoin a few lines.

The scene is clos'd, the curtain dropt,
    And famous Barry's part is o'er:
The music of that tongue is stopt,
    Which sooth'd and charm'd us heretofore!
Veil'd are those eyes, once piercing bright;
    Those rose-lips faded, late so red;
That once-fine form, unfit for sight,
    Laid low, to mingle with its bed!
Yet, tho' from earth's vain stage by Death now driv'n,
An Angel's part we trust she'll act in heav'n![21]

Acton church as Mrs. Barry would have known it, is no longer there. The present St. Mary's building dates from 1866, and at that time the church monuments were safely removed and installed in the new church.

---

[21] The Biographical Mirrour. London. Published by S. and E. Harding, Pall Mall. 1795. p. 30.

MRS ELIZABETH BARRY (1658-1713)

The monument to Mrs. Elizabeth Barry
in St. Mary's Church, Acton.

Due to enforced closures in 2020/21 of many institutions, it has not been possible to investigate who commissioned the monument. I have strong suspicions as to who it might have been, but my theory has yet to be proven. Hopefully, at some future date, that elusive person or persons will become known.

St. Mary's Church depicted in the 18th century, as Mrs. Barry would have known it, before its rebuilding in 1866.[22]

---

22 Records and Recollections of Acton by, Henry Mitchell. 1913.

MRS ELIZABETH BARRY (1658-1713)

Although intimated that Mrs. Barry's last performance was on the 8th of April 1709, in fact her last performance before her retirement took place on the 14th of April 1710, when she acted the Queen in *The Spanish Friar,* a tragicomedy by playwright and Poet Laureate John Dryden *(1631-1700),* at the Queen's Theatre, Haymarket. Also, Betterton's benefit took place on the 7th of April 1709, and not the 8th. Presumably, at this time, she was still living in St. Martin-in-the-Fields, as stated in the mill deed of 1706.

I often wondered as to the reason that Mrs. Barry, at the time of her retirement, moved from the heart of London to Acton, then a quiet rural village. But apparently Acton was, in the 17th century, a very pleasant place to reside, particularly after the discovery at that time of mineral springs at Acton Wells. The village became a popular country retreat for those of wealth from the City of London, with some having houses built there for country leisure. But later, owing to the vogue for Tunbridge Wells and Bath, Acton's popularity began to decline.

> Acton was held to be blessed with very sweet air in 1706 and the rector accordingly urged a friend, in verse, to move there. The fashion for medicinal waters brought a brief period of fame, with the exploitation of the wells at Old Oak common, when East Acton and Friars Place were said to be thronged with summer visitors, who had brought about improvement in the houses there.[23]

---

23 Diane K Bolton, Patricia E C Croot and M A Hicks, 'Acton: Growth', in *A History of the County of Middlesex: Volume 7, Acton, Chiswick, Ealing and Brentford, West Twyford, Willesden*, ed. T F T Baker and C R Elrington (London, 1982), pp. 7-14. *British History Online* http://www.british-history.ac.uk/vch/middx/vol7/pp7-14

Musings on Mrs. Elizabeth Barry and Her Friends

I believe the rector, who in 1706 urged his friend to move to Acton's *sweet air,* was a Richard Dewell, whose own monument can be seen in St. Mary's. Richard died in 1717 aged forty-seven and, according to the inscription, was the son of Timothy Dewell, Sacrae Theologiae Professor, late Rector of Lydiard Tregoze in Wiltshire. Timothy was born in 1616 and died in 1692. Richard was himself an alumnus of Magdelen College in Oxford, as were two of his brothers, Anthony and John, all following in the footsteps of their father, who matriculated there on the 13th of June 1634. Richard must have been the rector who presided over the interment of Mrs. Barry in 1713.

A simple twist of fate arises here. Timothy Dewell, who had been Rector of Lydiard Tregoze for forty-seven years, had been a close friend to Sir Walter St. John, 3rd Baronet *(1622-1708)* of Lydiard Tregoze, Wiltshire and of Battersea, and his wife Lady Johanna St. John *(1631-1705)*. Sir Walter was the brother of Anne St. John, whose second husband was Henry Wilmot, 1st Earl of Rochester, their son, the aforementioned infamous John Wilmot, 2nd Earl of Rochester, lover of Mrs. Barry. What a coincidence that Rector Richard Dewell would preside at the burial of the famous actress and that therefore his father, Timothy, would certainly have been aware of her liaison with Sir Walter's nephew.

In *Records and Recollections of Acton* by Henry Mitchell, 1913, there is also a poem regarding Acton's untainted air, by Dr. Cobden, Rector of Acton church from 1726. Dr. Cobden was Archdeacon of London and Chaplain to King George II:

> Some years previously, Dr. Cobden, Rector, writing probably to a newcomer, says:-

MRS ELIZABETH BARRY (1658-1713)

Since Providence is pleased to bless
Your state with plenty to excess.
And you can no provision want
Which Nature craves or Heaven can grant,
Give over all the busy care
Of gain, and with despatch repair
To Acton for untainted air;
There, happy in your rural seat,
Where nobles gladly might retreat,
Who, tho' in haste, their chariots stay,
Envying, yet pleased, while they survey
Those undisturbed in calm repose
Regain the health in town you lose.
Why with vexation should you waste
A life that hurries on too fast?
Why hardly breathe in stench and noise
When Paradise is in your choice?

Also in *Records and Recollections* is reference to another famous name of the theatre, that of Garrick. Mr. Nathan David Garrick came to live at Lichfield House, Acton, one of two adjoining brick houses, built in 1752. He was the great-great nephew of the famous actor David Garrick and in the house, over the fireplace in the dining-room, was proudly displayed Garrick's portrait by Zoffany.

***

The rare letter of Mrs. Barry's referred to earlier is held in the *Horace Howard Furness Memorial Library*, in the University of Pennsylvania. They have most kindly permitted inclusion of the image here. The letter was first published by Matthias Adam Shaaber *(1897-1979)* as *A*

Musings on Mrs. Elizabeth Barry and Her Friends

Letter from Mrs. Barry in *The Library Chronicle*. In the letter there is mention that; *only we have had pretty good success in the Opera of Rinaldo and Armida.* Although the letter is not dated, it has been said on good authority to have been written in 1699, the very year in which Dennis's opera *Rinaldo and Armida* was first performed. Mrs. Barry's letter was written to *The right Honourable the Lady Lisburne att her house att Troscod in Cardiganshire.* Lady Lisburne was Mallet Wilmot *(1676-1709),* who married John Vaughan, 1st Viscount Lisburne *(1667-1721)* in 1692. She was the youngest daughter of John Wilmot, Earl of Rochester, and she died at the young age of thirty-three, coincidently the same age as her father at *his* demise. This letter confirms that some nineteen years after John's death, when Mallet was twenty-three, she was a close friend of her late father's mistress, Mrs. Barry, who at that time was forty-one.

No matter all that has been documented about Elizabeth Barry's ancestral roots, whether a child of a father once of good estate or, as some might claim, of low parentage, this letter of Mrs. Barry's is certainly from an educated hand. Whether her learning was first gained at home or, as is believed, the outcome of Lady Mary Davenant's (formerly Henrietta Maria du Tremblay) educating we shall never know for sure. Lady Davenant was Sir William Davenant's third wife. She survived her husband by twenty-three years and was buried in the old vault at St. Bride's Church, Fleet Street, on the 24th of February 1690/1.

MRS ELIZABETH BARRY (1658-1713)

Madam

The pleasure I received in hearing from your Ladyship is impossible to be expressed and were my time as much in my power as my inclination I should be perpetually making use of the Honor your Ladyship has done me in permitting me to write to you I obeyed your Ladyships commands to Mr Batterton and Mrs Bracegirdle who return their humble service and thanks for soe great a favour; publick news is uncertain but I presume to give your Ladyship an account of a marriage and christ= ening in your family my Lord Baltomer's son was tuesday last married to my Lord Litchfield eldest daughter and my Lady Wharton is brought to bed of a son who is by my Lady Orford the Duke of Shrewsbury & my Lord Chancellour on friday next to be made a christian by the name of Philip as for the

Musings on Mrs. Elizabeth Barry and Her Friends

Little affairs of our house I never knew a worse winter only we have had pretty good success in the Opera of Rinaldo and Armida Where the poet made me command the Sea the earth and air but had I really that Authority I cou'd with joy forsake it all to wait on your Ladyship in your retirment which your Ladyships great goodness gives me hopes wou'd not be unwellcome to you I am with all submission

Madam

your Ladyships

I beg leave
to present my
humble service
to my Lord and wish
him and your Ladyship
many happy new years

Most obliged
and humble serv.'t

Lon: jan: y.e 30th
This moment Alexander
is bespoke to entertain y.e
and I mention'd to all their great honour

Eliza: Barry

MRS ELIZABETH BARRY (1658-1713)

Images: With kind permission from the University of Pennsylvania. Kislak Center for Special Collections - Manuscripts. Ms. Coll. 617.
Furness Autograph Collection. Folder 6

Transcription of the letter by M. A. Shaaber:

Musings on Mrs. Elizabeth Barry and Her Friends

Madam

The pleasure I received in hearing from your Ladyship is impossible to be expressed and were my time as much in my power as my inclination I shou'd be perpetually making use of the Honor your Ladyship has done me in permitting me to write to you I obeyed your Ladyships commands to Mr Batterton and Mrs Bracegirdle who returned their humble service and thanks for soe great a favour; publick news is uncertain but I presume to give your Ladyship an account of a marriage and christening in your family my Lord Baltomer's son was a tuesday last married to my Lord Litchfield Eldest Daughter and my Lady Wharton is brought to bed of a son who is by my Lady Orford the Duke of Shrewsbury & my Lord Chancellour on Friday next to be made a Christian by the name of Phillip as for the Little affairs of our house I never knew a worse [v°] Winter only we have had pretty good success in the Opera of Rinaldo and Armida Where the poet made me command the Sea the earth and Air but had I really that Authority I cou'd with joy forsake it all to wait on your Ladyship in your retirment which your Ladyships great goodness gives me hopes wou'd not be unwellcome to you I am with all submission

Madam
I beg Leave   Your Ladyships
to present my
humble Service

MRS ELIZABETH BARRY (1658-1713)

to my Lord and wish   Most Obliged
him and your Ladyship   and humble serv^t
Many happy new years

Lon: jan: ye 5th
This moment Alexander
is bespoke to entertain ye
Bride I mentioned &
  all their guest to-morrow   Eliza: Barry

The superscription reads:
ffor
    The Right Honorable the
    Lady Lisburne att her
    House att Troscod in
    Cardiganshire

                Salope post

Mongomery bagg[24]

Shaaber's observations on Mrs. Barry's letter.

> The letter is written on the second recto and verso of a sheet approximately 7 1/4" x 11 7/8", folded to make two leaves. The superscription is written on half of the first recto after the sheet has been folded once more. A wax seal is attached and the date (JA/5 in a circle) is

---

24   The Library Chronicle of the Friends of the University of Pennsylvania Library. Volume XVI. Fall 1949 – Summer 1950.

stamped above the address. Presumably the letter is an autograph.

The letter can be dated 1699 with assurance. According to the *Complete Peerage*, the son and heir of Lord Baltimore was married to the daughter of the Earl of Lichfield on 2 January 1699; according to the *Dictionary of National Biography*, Philip, the son of Lord Wharton, was born late in December 1698, and christened on the fifth of the month following.

The Lady Lisburne to whom the letter is addressed must be the wife of John Vaughan, Viscount Lisburne, of Trawscoed, co. Cardigan. As she was the daughter of the celebrated, or notorious, Earl of Rochester, she would appear to have kept up her father's patronage of the theater, for it was he who, according to report, introduced Mrs. Barry to the stage.

The persons mentioned in the letter, except for "Batterton" and Mrs. Bracegirdle, who are too well known to require comment, may be identified briefly.

"Lord Baltomer" is Charles Calvert, 3d Baron Baltimore (1637–1715), formerly governor of the colony of Maryland, and the bridegroom is the son who became the fourth baron for a few months after his father's death. He was about twenty-one at the time of the marriage. The bride was the daughter of the first Earl of Lichfield

MRS ELIZABETH BARRY (1658-1713)

and his wife, Lady Charlotte Fitzroy, an illegitimate daughter of Charles II. "My Lady Wharton" is Lucy, the second wife of Lord Wharton (subsequently the first Marquis of Wharton). The relationship implied by Mrs. Barry's phrase "in your family" is clear enough so far as the wedding is concerned: Lady Lisburne's grandmother was also the grandmother of the Earl of Lichfield. After surviving her first husband, Sir Francis Henry Lee, Bart., to whom she had borne Lichfield's father, she married the first Earl of Rochester and became the mother of the most eminent holder of that title. But what link between Rochester and Lord Wharton Mrs. Barry had in mind is uncertain. Lord Wharton's first wife (Anne Wharton, the poetess) was also a granddaughter of Sir Francis Henry Lee and his spouse, but that relationship seems immaterial to the occasion. It is also true that Lord Wharton's second wife was the daughter of Adam Loftus, Viscount Lisburne, but his title became extinct upon the death at the siege of Limerick in 1691; the husband of Rochester's daughter was Viscount Lisburne by a creation of 5 June 1695. I have discovered no kinship between the last and present holder of the title.

Lady Orford is the wife of Edward Russell, first Earl of Orford (1652–1727), better known perhaps as Admiral Russell, the victor at La Hogue. The Duke of Shrewsbury is Charles Talbot, the first duke (1660–1718). The lord chancellor is the celebrated Lord Somers (1651–1716). Mrs. Barry's list of sponsors, however, seems incorrect, possibly because of a subsequent change of plan; according to Narcissus Luttrell (iv. 469), the king and the Duke of Shrewsbury were the godfathers and the Princess Anne the godmother. The duke, the lord chancellor, and Lord Orford were all political allies of Lord Wharton, a sporting peer who was at this time comptroller of the royal household. The boy about to be baptized under such august auspices turned out to be the rakehell Duke of Wharton.

There is a slight discrepancy between the dates given by Mrs. Barry for the marriage and the baptism and those given by the *Complete Peerage* and the *D.N.B.* (2d,5th). In 1699, 5 January fell on a Thursday; "tuesday last" would therefore be the third and "friday next" the following day, the sixth. The fact that Mrs. Barry first dated her letter the fourth and then wrote a 5 over the numeral sheds no light on this point. It is hard to say which witness is the more likely to be wrong.

Of the plays which Mrs. Barry mentions, *Rinaldo and Armida* is an "opera," *i.e.,* a tragedy

MRS ELIZABETH BARRY (1658-1713)

with a generous allotment of incidental music, by John Dennis. It was probably brought out at Lincoln's Inn Fields early in the current season; it was printed in 1699. Mrs. Barry played Armida to Betterton's Rinaldo. If there could be any doubt about the identification, it would be dispelled by the fact that the poet does give Armida command over the elements and indeed over the infernal regions, a proviso Mrs. Barry forgot to mention to Lady Lisburne (pp.15f.):

And thou, O Air, that murmur'st on the Mountain,
Be hush'd at my command, silence ye Winds,
That make outrageous War upon the Ocean;
And thou, old Ocean, lull thy wond'ring Waves;
Ye Warring Elements be hush'd as Death,
While I impose my Dread Commands on Hell.

"Alexander" I take to be *The Rival Queens, or, the Death of Alexander the Great*, by Nathaniel Lee, a favorite of long-standing frequently mentioned by its alternative title. One would not think it eminently suitable to a wedding, but then there is the precedent of a tragedy of Pyramus and Thisbe to give one pause.

The contents of Mrs. Barry's letter, which so far as I can learn has never before been printed, are of moderate interest only, but it deserves notice as a memento of a great actress of an era

Musings on Mrs. Elizabeth Barry and Her Friends

whose actresses did not leave many mementos of this kind behind them. I may add that, if Mrs. Barry compose the letter herself, she wrote with a fluency which is a little surprising, and that, while she almost completely disdains punctuation, her spelling is remarkably modern.

It is interesting to note Mrs. Barry's personal wax seal attached to her letter. As far as I can see, it looks like the shape of an eye at the top, with at least six tear drops falling beneath. I'm not sure what all this represents, but Mrs. Barry *was* the most accomplished tragedienne of her day... could her seal have represented this?

PART TWO

TOWN MILLS, NEWBURY

It has been said that Mrs. Barry had been associated with various lovers during her lifetime. However, I believe the last of them could have been the aforementioned Gabriel Ballam who, in Mrs. Barry's will, had been left her *Estate at Newbury consisting of mills.*

Town Mills at Newbury proved not to be elusive in themselves, as there is a photograph of them taken in the late 19th century when they were rebuilt after a fire, and in modern times they were apparently developed into flats. Finding proof of Elizabeth Barry's ownership of the lease was a little more tricky, owing to the sparse reference to them in her will. And the will of John Ballam of Wadham College gave me that ever-looked-for *Eureka* moment. In his will he states the following:

> ...Item I give unto the Reverend M^r. Richard Peers of Berks aforesaid all that my Leasehold Estate held of the Dean and Cannons of Windsor called the Town Mills situate lying and being in Newbury in the County of Berks to hold to him the said M^r. Richard Peers his Executors and administrators and Assigns...[25]

This was the unexpected result of a piece of research which proves that the Town Mills referred to in John Ballam's

---

[25] Will of John Ballam, Master of Arts of Wadham College. PROB 11/629/289.The National Archives.

Town Mills, Newbury

will were in fact the mills that had been bequeathed to Gabriel Ballam by Mrs. Barry.

The original medieval Town Mills, together with lands and tenement, were first leased by the Dean and Canons of Windsor to John Knyght of Newbury, gentleman and Walter Collyns of Newbury, mercer, on the 20th of June 1540. The properties were then leased to various people throughout the 17th century between 1605 and 1698, on which latter date Mary Kelloway, widow, took the lease following the death of her husband, John Kelloway, miller, who had been the lessee from 1683. After eight years, the widow relinquished her interest in the property and Mrs. Barry became the new lessee of Town Mills on the 4th of November 1706. I obtained a copy of the lease from St. George's Chapel Archives & Chapter Library but sadly, due to some age damage of the deed, parts are illegible. Thankfully though, an excellent description of the lease has been documented by St. George's Chapel Archives:

> Lease by the Dean and Canons of Windsor to Elizabeth Barry of St Martin's in the Fields, Middx.,of (1) their water mills in Newbury, together with the piece of land called Floodgates belonging thereto; (2) one little plot of land called the Withy bed; and (3) a tenement in Bartholomew Street, Newbury then in the occupation of Robert Banninge; for a term of 21 years from Michaelmas 1706, at the yearly rents of (a) £10 16s.(i.e., for the water mills and floodgates £10 1s.; for the withy bed 1s. 8d.; and for the tenement 13. 4d.); and (b) two couple of capons (or 10s. at the election of the Lessors' Steward for the time being); all payable by two

MRS ELIZABETH BARRY (1658-1713)

equal instalments at Lady Day and Michaelmas in each year. Covenants by the Lessee: (i) to keep and yield up the demised premises in repair; (ii) that the Lessors or their officer might enter the demised premises to view any lack of repair, the Lessee being required to amend the same within one year of being notified thereof; (iii) to pay, and to indemnify the Lessors in respect of all quitrents and other payments, duties and charges, both ordinary and extraordinary, due or payable out of or for the demised premises during the term thereby granted; (iv) not to alienate the demised premises (except by will) without the prior consent under seal of the Lessors; and (v) that any person to whom such alienation should have been made was to surrender the Lease within one year of such alienation and take a new Lease of the premises for the then unexpired term of this Lease but otherwise upon similar terms and conditions. Proviso that if the rent of £10 16s. should have remained unpaid for 30 days after becoming payable, or if the Lessee should have failed to repair the demised premises within one year after having been given notice so to do, or if the Lessee should have alienated the demised premises (except by will) without the prior consent under seal of the Lessors, or if any alienee should have failed to take a new Lease as aforesaid, then the term thereby granted should cease and be determined. Witnesses to the execution of the Counterpart by the Lessee: Mary Hollaway, William Pepper &

Town Mills, Newbury

> Richard Barrow. Lease & Counterpart each bear Stamp Duty of 1s.[26]

Gabriel Ballam died of consumption and was buried at St. Giles, Cripplegate in London on the 28th of December 1715, with his brother John administering his estate as Gabriel had not made a will. John then took on the lease of the mills in his own right, granted to him by the Dean and Canons of Windsor, on the 4th of December 1716.

> Lease by the Dean and Canons of Windsor to John Ballam of Wadham College, Oxford, administrator of the estate of his brother Gabriel Ballam, deceased...[27]

Then, on the 20th of November 1723, a renewal lease of the mills was taken out by John Ballam, and on his death, in May 1729, the lease passed to Reverend Richard Peers of Faringdon in Berkshire. Richard was born in the parish of All Saint's, Oxford on the 15th of July 1685. He matriculated from Trinity College, Oxford on the 3rd of December 1701, and was elected scholar there in 1702, gaining a B.A. in 1705 and an M.A. three years later. In 1710 he became Vicar of Hartley-Wintney in Hampshire until 1711 when he became Vicar of Faringdon in Berkshire, and continued there until his death on the 20th of July 1739. Richard was author of three works; *The Character of an Honest Dissenter in Twelve Marks* Oxford,

---

26 Newbury, Berkshire. Lease of mills. 4 November 1706. Reference Number. SGC XV.29.14. St George's Chapel Archives & Chapter Library. Windsor Castle, College of St. George.

27 Newbury, Berkshire. Lease of mills. 4 December 1716. Reference Number. SGC XV.29.16. St George's Chapel Archives & Chapter Library. Windsor Castle, College of St. George.

MRS ELIZABETH BARRY (1658-1713)

1715, with further editions of 1717 and 1718; *The Great Tendency of the Positive Precepts of the Gospel, to Promote the Observance of Natural Religion.* London, 1731 and *A Companion for the Aged...* London, 1722, published in many editions, the fourteenth being by the Society for Promoting Christian Knowledge in 1823.

Richard was the executor of John Ballam's will dated the 20th of January 1728/9, John dying just four months after. Reverend Peers enjoyed rewards from the lease of Town Mills through John's bequest and then, on the 11th of July 1737, took on the lease for himself.

Reverend Peers died intestate in 1739, at the age of fifty-four, leaving his widow, Dorothy, as the administratrix of his estate, though it was apparently left unadministered. With Dorothy's demise in 1744, a kinsman, Reverend Henry Peers of Newington in Kent became the administrator of *her* estate, which included her husband's lease of the mills. Consequently, Henry then became the new lessee from the 3rd of January 1744.

> Lease by the Dean and Canons of Windsor to Revd Henry Peers of Newington, Kent, clerk, administrator of the estate of Dorothy Peers, deceased (who was the widow and administratrix of the estate of Revd Richard Peers) and also administrator of the estate of Revd Richard Peers which had been unadministered by Dorothy Peers (in consideration, inter alia, of the surrender of an earlier Lease granted to Revd Richard Peers)...[28]

---

[28] Newbury, Berkshire. Lease of mills. 3 January 1744. Reference Number. SGC XV.29.19. St George's Chapel Archives & Chapter Library. Windsor Castle, College of St. George.

PART THREE

GABRIEL BALLAM'S FAMILY ROOTS

Gabriel Ballam was baptised on the 6th of February 1672/3 at Saint Saviour, Southwark. He was the second son of four born to Jonadab and Patience Ballam, who were married on the 6th of November 1664 at St. Olave's Church, Southwark.

Gabriel's father was christened on the 20th of January 1631 at Bengeworth, in Worcestershire. He was the son of John Ballam, born *(c.1580)* who, in 1600, was Master of Evesham School. John then became the Curate of St. Lawrence Church there and, by 1610, was made its Minister. John died in September 1639, after making his will on the 19th of April that year, with probate proved on the 15th of November following. There is no mention of a wife; presumably she had died before him, leaving him with two sons, John his elder and Jonadab his younger. He also had three daughters, namely Mary, Martha and Pheobe. The will took the usual form, the elder son first benefiting from rents and profits of his father's property and land in Evesham, held in trust for him after his father's demise, to be administered by the will's trustees and executors. Substantial amounts from such rents and profits gained were to be paid to the testator's remaining children. It appears that John became a student at New Inn Hall on the 26th of June 1635 at the age of seventeen, he gaining a B.A. in January 1638/9 and an M. A. in January 1641/2. It is believed that he became Rector of Wittersham, Kent in 1647 and Vicar of Damerham, Wiltshire in 1658. On John's death, the said payments became the responsibility of his young brother, Jonadab. John Ballam's will also bequeathed sums of money to a servant and the poor of the parishes of Bengeworth and St. Lawrence, with household items bequeathed to the children, such as feather beds, a ring, silver plate etc.

Gabriel's father, Jonadab, was only seven years old at his father's demise, but by the age of fifteen was apprenticed, on the 20th June 1646, as Clerk to John Keeble, a citizen of the Grocers' Company. He eventually rose to establish his own grocery business in Southwark, no doubt with the help of his father's wealth. Later, Jonadab became a member of the Grocers' Company, established in 1345 and one of the Twelve Great City Livery Companies.

By 1683, Jonadab was a member of the Grand-Jury for the Town and Borough of Southwark. His name appears on a Presentment, with many other jury members, regarding the *Rye House Plot* of 1683:

> **The PRESENTMENT of the Grand-Jury for the Town and Borough of Southwark in the County of Surrey, and divers other adjacent Places in the same County, at the General Sessions of the Peace holden for the said Town and Borough, &c. at the Bridghouse-Hall within the said Borough, on Friday the 27th. of June, in the Six and Thirtieth year of the Reign of our Sovereign Lord CHARLES the Second by the Grace of God King of England, Scotland, France and Ireland, Defender of the Faith, &c.**
>
> There having been lately detected a Horrid Conspiracy, against the Lives of the King and

the Duke of York, the established Government of Church and State, and the Liberties of the English Nation: We do Present the said Conspiracy to be still manifestly carried on; as appears by the Practices of the Republican, and Fanatical Faction: And likewise, by the Declarations of some of the Conspirators themselves at the place of Execution: Holloway, particularly, delivering himself in his Confession and Narrative, in these very words, There would be no want of Men, if it (speaking of the Insurrection) were once begun. And afterward, If we should name every one that we thought would be concerned, I believe we might name three parts of London. Giving therein to understand, that they expected as well to be seconded by those that were only Well-willers to the Cause, as by others that were Actually engaged in the Malice of the Design.

We do therefore Present, as our Opinion, that all those, who either by Open favour, or Connivence, Directly or Indirectly, by Word, Counsel, or Action, give Countenance, or Encouragement, to any Seditious or Schismatical Disturbers of the Publick Peace, are, and ought to be comprized within the number of the aforesaid Well-willers to the interest of that Cause and Party.

And we do the rather Present, and humbly Recommend this to consideration; in regard of the many Frauds, and Artifices, that are commonly made use of for the Inveigling of the

MRS ELIZABETH BARRY (1658-1713)

credulous Multitude, seducing the Ignorant; corrupting the Vain, and improving all occasions and ill humors, toward the dishonour both of the King and of the Church, and the embroiling of the Government.

And whereas it has been the constant Method of these Turbulent Spirits, as well in printed Libels, and written News-Letters, as in their ordinary Discourses, to Revile and Slander the King, and the Church; to Calumniate his Majesties Ministers of State and Justice, and all Loyal Subjects, that out of a sense of Conscience, and Duty, have either Acted, spoken, or written, in Defence of the Government, Ecclesiastical and Civil; and for the undeceiving of his Majesties Liege People: By means whereof, they have endeavoured, as much as in them lay, not only to blast the Memory of all honest men, but even to stigmatize Virtue and Loyalty it self.

In contemplation of these Outrages against Humanity, Duty, good Manners, and common Justice; We do Present, as our further Opinion, the necessity of fixing some publick Mark of Infamy, upon all scandalous and seditious, printed Books, Pamphlets and Papers, of the Quality above mentioned, to prevent the transmitting of so many Honourable Names, with Infamy, to Posterity.

We do likewise Present, that Factious Coffee-men, Victuallers, and Ale-house-Keepers in this Borough, have greatly contributed to our late

Divisions; and that divers of them do still continue to make their Houses the Receptacles of Disloyal and ill-affected Persons in suspicious numbers: Notwithstanding their entire dependence upon his Majesties Grace and Bounty, for the Livelihood of Themselves, and their Families.

In which regard, we Present it needful, that some effectual course be taken with them, either for their suppression, or their better behaviour for the future.

> Jonadab Ballam.
> Edward Collingwood.
> John Gerard.
> Henry Durnford.
> Benjamin Chapman.
> Robert Sparks.
> William Duke.
> Francis Walker.
> Martin Gray, sen.
> George Bickers.
> John Hall.
> John Crosse.
> Charly Stanton.
> William Greening.
> Richard Snart.
> William Smith.
> William Wornham.

> Villa & Burgus de *Southwark* necnon di|vers. Paroch. & loci in|fra Com.

MRS ELIZABETH BARRY (1658-1713)

Surr. Ad General. Quarterial. Session. pacis Dom. Regis tent. pro Villa & Burgo de *Southwark,* ac in & per tot. Parochias S. Olavi, S. Thomae, S. Salvat. S. Georgii, ac in *Kentstreet, Blackmanstreet* in Paroch. de *Newington* in Com. *Surr.* apud le *Bridghouse* infra Villam & Burg. praedict. in Com. praedict. die Veneris scil. vicesimo septimo die Junii, Anno Regni Reg. Caroli Secund. nunc Angliae, &c. tricesimo sexto.

It is ordered by this Court that the Presentment of the Grand Inquest, now here delivered and openly read, be forthwith Printed by *Benjamin Tooke.*

Wagstaffe.[29]

The Rye House Plot was a conspiracy to assassinate King Charles II *(1630-1685)* and his brother James, Duke of York *(1633-1701)* on their way back to London after attending the Newmarket races in April of that year. In a fortuitous twist of fate, a devastating fire broke out in the town of Newmarket on the 22nd of March and consequently the races were cancelled, with the King and Duke returning earlier than planned. Many people were implicated in the plot, including several prominent Whigs. Executions, imprisonments and exiles followed. It is believed that one of the leading conspirators was the King's illegitimate son,

---

29 https://quod.lib.umich.edu/e/eebo/A55731.0001.001/1:1?rgn=div1;view=fulltext

Gabriel Ballam's Family Roots

James Scott, 1st Duke of Monmouth and 1st Duke of Buccleuch *(1649-1685)*, later beheaded for his part in the Monmouth Rebellion.

Extract from *A True Account and Declaration of The Horrid Conspiracy Against the Late King, His Present Majesty, and the Government: As it was Ordered to be Published by His late Majesty....1685*, indicating where the unspeakable assassination would have taken place:

A particular Account of the Situation of the
Rye-House.

The *Rye-House* in *Hartfordshire,* about eighteen Miles from *London,* is so called from the *Rye* a Meadow near it. Just under it there is a By-road from *Bishops-Strafford* to *Hoddesden,* which was constantly used by the King when he went to or from *Newmarket*; the great Road winding much about on the Right-hand by *Stansted.* The House is an Old Strong Building and stands alone, encompass'd with a Mote, and towards the Garden has high Walls, so that Twenty Men might easily defend it for some time against Five hundred. From a high Tower in the House all that go or come may be seen both ways for near a Mile distance. As you come from *Newmarket* towards *London,* when you are near the House, you pass the Meadow over a narrow Caus-way, at the end of which is a Toll-gate, which having Entred you go through a Yard, and a little Field, and at the end of that through another Gate, you pass into a narrow

MRS ELIZABETH BARRY (1658-1713)

Lane, where two Coaches at that time could not go a-breast. This narrow Passage had on the Left hand a thick Hedge and a Ditch, on the Right a long Range of Building used for Corn Chambers and Stables with several Doors and Windows looking into the Road, and before it a Pale, which then made the Passage so narrow, but is since removed. When you are past this long Building, you go by the Mote, and the Garden Wall, that is very Strong, and has divers Holes in it, through which a great many Men might shoot. Along by the Mote and Wall the Road continues to the *Ware-River* which runs about Twenty or Thirty yards from the Mote, and is to be past by a Bridge. A small distance from thence another Bridge is to be past over the *New-River*. In both which Passes a few Men may oppose great Numbers. In the outer Court-yard, which is behind the long Building, a considerable Body of Horse and Foot might be drawn up unperceived from the Road; whence they might easily issue out at the same time into each end of the narrow Lane, which was also to be stopt up by overturning a Cart.

On the 18th of July 1687, during the reign of James II, Jonadab was appointed along with six others, to serve as Warden of the Company of Grocers and remained so until the 15th of October that year, when the Wardens were removed from office by Order of the King in Council. They were re-elected by the 1st of July 1689 under William III *(1650-1702)*, on which date Jonadab Ballam was excused from serving on paying a fine of twenty-five pounds.

Gabriel Ballam's Family Roots

Jonadab was a man of some importance in the parish of Southwark, for as well as a Warden of the Company of Grocers, he was Treasurer of St. Saviour's Free Grammar School and various receipts were paid to him from April 1689 to February 1689/90.

At London Metropolitan Archives, from the Bridge House Estates collection Reference: CLA/007/EM/03/228, there is an *Indenture of a Lease by Jonadab Ballam 1691 to a John Langley of eight acres of ground, being parcel of Moulton's Close in the parish of St. George the Martyr, Southwark.* And in the same collection under Reference: CLA/007/EM/03/141 there is an interesting Bond of Mary Kirby of Wakefield, Yorkshire, widow, and Jonadab Ballam, citizen and grocer of London 1678. *To indemnify the Mayor and Commonalty against all claims in virtue of the lease granted to Francis Kirby, late husband of the said Mary, of a tenement on the East side of the North end of London Bridge; upon the destruction of which in the late fire...*

Jonadab was also one of the benefactors on the commencement of the building of St. Thomas's Hospital, Southwark, in 1693.

***

Born into wealth, little appears to be known of the occupation, if any, of Gabriel Ballam, but from evidence so far researched he appears to have been a man of leisure and acquainted with contemporary poets, playwrights and dramatists. A frequenter of the famous Will's Coffee House in Covent Garden, Gabriel appeared to be one of its witty patrons, with the poet, playwright and first Laureate, John Dryden *(1631-1700)*, the centre of attraction for their

MRS ELIZABETH BARRY (1658-1713)

gatherings. Such a circle of playwright and dramatist friends could point to Gabriel's friendship with Mrs. Barry.

On Jonadab's death, aged seventy-seven, in 1702, Richard Ballam took over his father's grocery business, his mother having died seven years earlier. Sadly, however, the eldest son's gaining of the business was short lived as he died just four years after on the 2nd of January 1706/7 at the age of forty.

Will of Jonadab Ballam:

> **In the Name of God Amen** This tenth day of August one thousand seven hundred and two And in the first year of the raign of our Soveraign Lady Anne of England Scotland France and Ireland Queen defender of the Faith I Jonadab Ballam of Southwarke in the County of Surrey Grocer being in good health and sound and perfect memory through God's grace and mercy but in regard of the frailty and uncertainty of this transitory Life Do therefoure make and Declare this to be my last Will and Testament in manner and forme following (Viz^t) First and principally I committ my soul into the hands of Almighty God my Maker and Creator and of his Sonn Jesus Christ my only Saviour and Redeemer through the above merritts of whose most pretious death and passion I steadfastly hope to be saved My Body to the earth from where it came desireing to be decently and privately buryed in the parish church of S^t. Saviours in Southwarke And I Do hereby order that my Executors hereafter named shall not

exceed or expend above Fourscore pounds at my Funerall And as to my real Estate I Do give and Dispose of as followeth Imprimis I Do give and bequeath unto my eldest Sonn Richard Ballam All my Lands in Swanscome in the County of Kent now in the possession and tenure of Henry or John Acourt alias Gardner his under Tenants or Assignes And alsoe all the woods thereunto belonging standing and growing now in my owne hands And likewise all the Timber and Timberlike Trees reserved in their lease to him and his Heires of his Body lawfully begotten And for want of such issue the said Richard Ballam shall and may Dispose of all the said Lands and Woods unto some or any one of my children that shall then survive or unto any his Sister Patience Ballam or her Heires Provided nonetheless that the said Richard Ballam shall Declare the same in Writing by his last Will and Testament lawfully published in the presence of three Witnesses And for want of such Will and Testament or for want of such issue I do give the said Lands and Woods in Swanscome aforesaid unto my youngest Sonn John Ballam and unto his heire forever Item I give and bequeath unto my youngest Sonn John Ballam all my Lands in Holden in the County of Kent now in the tenure and occupation of Thomas Lewes his under Tenants or Assigns To him and the heires of his Body lawfully begotten And for want of such issue I do give and bequeath unto my eldest son Rich: Ballam all the said Lands in Holden aforesaid unto him and his Heires for ever And

MRS ELIZABETH BARRY (1658-1713)

as to my personall Estate according the custom and freedome of the City of London my Debts and Funeral charges being paid and Discharged I Dispose of the one moyety or halfe part as followeth Item I give to Sister Marshall tenn pounds to M^r. Thomas Andrew tenn pounds to Sr Gabriel Roberts ten pounds to my Lady Roberts tenn pounds and to Dr Samuel Bouton ten pounds all four mourning Item I give to poor of S^t. Saviours within the Borough Liberty fifteen pounds to be disposed of by the Churchwardens for the time being at or upon the second day of February next after my decease Item I give unto my eldest Sonn Richard Ballam out of the moyety or halfe part of my said personall Estate at my owne Disposall all my stock in the joint trade between us which upon casting up Shop at Christmas one thousand seven Hundred was Fifteen Hundred pounds but be more or less I give it him entirely he paying and Discharging all Debts due to me or any other person out of the said joint stock in trade that shall be due at the time of my decease Item I Do give unto my loving Daughter Patience Ballam All my Stock in the Bank of England being Seven Hundred and Fifty pounds with all the perquisites advantages and Dividents thereunto growing and belonging to be transferred by my executor whereafter named within three Months after my Decease to her or unto Trustees for her only use and benefit And for the choice of such Trustees I recommend unto her S^r. Gabriel Roberts and Doctor Samuel Bouton desiring that they would assist her in her affaires with their advice and counsell Item I do alsoe give unto my eldest Sonn Richard Ballam and to my Daughter Patience Ballam all my Plate and Rings that were mine at the time of my Decease to be Divided equally between them And in consideration thereof they shall pay to their Brothers Jonadab Gabriel and John Ballam Five pounds each apeece There is a Debt of one Hundred and Fifty pounds due to me from Sonn Jondab Ballam the particulars and in my old Debt Book Sett: 366 And also another debt due to me on several Bonds from Sonn Gabriel Ballam of two Hundred Ninety one pounds Fourteen Shillings which they have extravagantly Spent since they were of the age of Twenty and one years and which said Debts are over and above the large allowances I have made them quarterly for their Subsistence and Maintenance which said severall Debts my executors hereafter named may Deduct out of their shares and proportions or Release to them the said Debts as they shall see cause or as they behave themselves towards them my said Executors the other Moyety or halfe part of my said personall Estate I do give to my Four children Jonadab Gabriel John and Daughter Patience Ballam to be proportioned into four parts share and share alike And in part of such shares or Divident Gabriel Ballam shall have the reversion of an Annuity purchased by his grand Father only for his Life and to make up his Life Ninety Nine years from Xmas one thousand six

MRS ELIZABETH BARRY (1658-1713)

Hundred Ninety Five I paid sixty three pounds so that he shall have the possession and reversion for sixty three pounds as it cost me seven years since in p^{tt} of his share or Divident and John Ballam my youngest Sonn shall have the possession and reversion of another Annuity which I purchased for his Life first for one Hundred pounds and afterwards to make up his life Ninety Nine years from Xmas one thousand six Hundred Ninety Five I paid into the Kings Exchequer sixty three pounds seven years since soe that he shall have the possession and reversion of Fourteen pounds per Annum to be paid quarterly for one Hundred Sixty three pounds as it cost me in part of his share or Divident of the fourth part of the Moyety of my said personall Estate And lastly I do make constitute and appoint my eldest Sonn Richard Ballam and John Ballam my youngest Sonn to be executors of this my last Will and Testament And I do hereby revoke all former or other Wills whatever by me made or spoken and none to stand and be in force but this my last Will and Testament only In Witness whereof to this my last Will and Testament containing one only sheet of paper I have set to my hand and have affixed my Seale the day and year first above written Jonadab Ballam Signed Sealed published and declared by me the Testator as and for my last Will and Testament in the

Gabriel Ballam's Family Roots

presence of Ben: Newington John Gater W^m. Matthews John <Towell>[30]

As can be seen from the will, Gabriel and his brother Jonadab seems to have been solely reliant on their father's generosity for subsistence and maintenance *which they have extravagantly spent since they were of the age of 21 years*. The two of them appeared to have been spendthrifts, unlike their hard working older brother, Richard, and their younger brother, John of whom more will be said later.

The following verses and inscriptions in St. Saviour's Southwark (now Southwark Cathedral) were noted by the antiquary and natural philosopher John Aubrey *(1626-1697)* on his perambulation of Surrey during the 1670s and 1690s. His observations were later published as *The Natural History and Antiquities of the County of Surrey Vol. V, 1719*:

On a Stone under the Arms of the Company of *Grocers* were these Verses.

GARRET *some call him, but that was to high;*
His Name is GARRARD, *who now here doth lye:*
He in his Youth was toss'd with many a Wave,
But now at Port arrived, rests in his Grave.
The Church he did frequent whilst he had Breath,
And wish'd to lye therein after his Death;
Weep not for him, since he is gone before
To Heaven, where GROCERS *there are many more.*

On a greyish Grave-Stone is this fol-

---
[30] Will of Jonadab Ballam, Grocer of Southwark. PROB 11/466/409. The National Archives

MRS ELIZABETH BARRY (1658-1713)

lowing inscription;

> JONADAB BALLAM *obiit* 25 *Octobris*
> *Anno Ætatis suæ* 77°
> *Anno Domini* 1702.
> PATIENCE BALLAM *his wife, obiit* 25
> Marcii *Anno Ætatis suæ* 55°
> *Annoq; Domini* 1695
> RICHARDUS BALLAM (1) *Natu maximus*
> *Obiit* 2 Jan. 1706. *Ætat* 40.

(1) Sic Orig

Richard Ballam made his Will on the 13th of December 1705, in perfect mind and memory. No sickness of body is mentioned, so we can perhaps assume he was in reasonable health at the time his will was drawn up, although he died unexpectedly only twenty days after.

> **In the Name of God Amen** I Richard Ballam of St Saviours Southwarke in the County of Surrey grocer being of sound and perfect mind and memory Do make this my last Will and Testament in manner and form following Viz^t Imprimis I bequeath my Soul to God who gave it hoping for salvation through the merritts and mediation of Jesus Christ his only Sonn our Saviour and Redeemer my body I commit to the Earth from where it came and as to my Worldly Estate I give devise and bequeath the same as followes Item I give devise and bequeath to my youngest Brother John Ballam and to his Heires all my Lands Tenements and Hereditaments

Gabriel Ballam's Family Roots

situate lying and being in Swanscombe in the County of Kent now in the tenure or occupation of Henry or John Acourt alias Gardiner his Undertenant or Assignes And alsoe all the Woods Timber and Timber like Trees thereunto belonging now in my owne hands with their and every of their appurtenances and all other my Lands Tenements and Hereditaments whatsoever lying and being in Swanscombe afores^d or else where in the County of Kent To hold to my said Brother John Ballam his Heires and Assignes for ever Item I give and bequeath unto John Lade Esqr of the Borough of Southwarke aforesaid the summe of twenty pounds of lawful money of England To the Reverend Mr Thomas Horne one of the Chaplains of St Saviours Southwarke I give twenty pounds of like lawful money To the poor of the Borough Side of the parish of St Saviours Southwarke aforesaid I give the summe of fifteen pounds of like money to be distributed amongst them by the Churchwardens of the said Parish for the time being on the twenty sixth day of November next after my Decease To poor housekeepers to be distributed amongst them by the aforesaid Mr Lade and Mr Horne I give the summe of twenty pounds To John <Towel> I give the sum of tenn pounds to buy him mourning and a Ring besides Item I give to my brother Jonadab Ballam the sum of twenty pounds Item I give to my Brother Gabriell Ballam twenty pounds Lastly I give devise and bequeath all the rest and residue of my Estate both reall and personall to my youngest Brother John Ballam And I make him the Executor of this my last Will and Testament In Witness whereof I have hereunto set my hand and Seal this thirteenth day of December anno Din one thousand seven hundred and five Richard Ballam Signed sealed published and declared by the said Richard Ballam the Testator for his last Will and Testament in the presence of us who then subscribed our Names as Witnesses thereto in his presence after interlining those words (Brother besides) in two several places Magnus Byne Jn°. Gater Tho: Rous[31]

It seems from Richard's generous bequests to his youngest brother, John, that his other brothers, Jonadab and Gabriel, had made their way in the world and as such had accumulated wealth in their own right. On the other hand, there may have been a family dispute in which Richard felt less favourable towards these two brothers, hence the relatively meagre bequests of twenty pounds in comparison with John Ballam's future income from the lands and timber reserves in Swanscombe, Kent. John Ballam, the fortunate legatee of the lands had, at the age of sixteen in 1691/2, entered Wadham College, Oxford, gaining a B.A. in 1695 and an M.A. three years later. He was restored to the college on the 25th of June 1729 to Richard Peers.

John, having no heirs or assigns himself, bequeathed at his death in 1731 the Swanscombe lands together with lands and buildings in High Halden in Kent to the Reverend Richard Peers of Faringdon, Berkshire.

---

[31] Will of Richard Ballam, Grocer of Saint Saviour Southwark, Surrey. The National Archives. PROB 11/492/78

PART FOUR

GABRIEL BALLAM'S FRIENDS

My conjecture on Gabriel Ballam being Mrs. Barry's lover stems from remarks in certain letters written to and from him c.1698, when Mrs. Barry was still a player on the Stage. Correspondence between Ballam and his friend Anthony Smith M.A. of Cambridge, who died at Newport Pagnell in Buckinghamshire in 1721 aged forty-nine, suggests that they were in discussion regarding the censorious *Short View of the Immorality and Profaneness of the English Stage (1698)*. This work was by Jeremy Collier *(1650-1726)*, theatre critic, non-juror bishop and theologian, which leads to the thought that Gabriel was a keen patron of the playhouse:

To Mr. Gabriel Ballam: *To be left at* Will's *Coffee-house* in Covent-garden.

Sir,
Tho' I have been under the Scene of Silence, yet now, I appear to pay my Promise to him that can forgive: To make an Apology, is Effeminate; or to tell Business was the Cause, is Threadbare: And therefore, I confess I have committed a Soloecism in Friendship; and send this Sheet to do Penance. To furnish you with News, I cannot; and to tell you *Cambridge* Jests, that's Foreign; since they, like their Learning, are confin'd only to their own Meridian: To tell you their Disputes

in Divinity, is altogether as strange, since that's out of your Sphere, and consequently must Affront, rather than oblige you: but to add something for your Two Pence, *Collier's* Book is greedily swallow'd, and all your little carping, envious Answers, are, like their Authors, scandalous. D—— is the most rejected, since his Book answers not his Title, nor his Title Mr. Collier's. Mr. *V——ook* is not yet descanted on, since its Arrival is not of a Day. I can't furnish you with more Lines now, since I am going to be Cap'd Master of Arts; therefore beg your Excuse till I arrive at *Newport-Pagnel*, whither I gang on *Thursday*.

Your Assured Friend,

Anthony Smith[32]

Gabriel's witty reply to Smith's letter:

> To Mr. Anthony Smith, *M.A.*

> *Sir,*
> Your learned *Cambridge* Epistle I receiv'd with no common Satisfaction; for truly, Sir, it carries that Air of a Philosophy-Lecture, that I cannot fancy any thing less, than that you have

---

[32] A Pacquet from Will's: Or a New Collection of Original Letters on several subjects;...Written and collected by several hands. London. Printed for Sam. Briscoe, and sold by John Nutt near Stationers-Hall, 1701. pp.42-43

honoured me with some Part of your Exercise that Cap'd you with your New Title of Master of Arts. I confess, you happy University-Gentlemen, with your seven Years Labour amongst Books and Letters, arrived to the Crowning your Heads with that Honourable Cap; and then, in half a dozen Years more, amongst Men and Manners here in *London*, you fill them with brains to: For indeed you Politick Architects of Literature, wisely Roof first and then Floor, Finish, and Furnish afterwards

I assure you, Sir, you have no occasion of doing Penance in a Sheet, as you call your Letter; and I less of giving you your own dear Collier's Blessing, viz. ABSOLUTION. And now I talk of that famous Author, whose Book you tell me is so greedily swallow'd amongst you, I am afraid your *Cambridge* Swallow is better than your Digestion, and that Mr. *Collier* slips down with you like an Eel through a Cormorant; for otherwise, if you would give your selves the leisure of chewing upon it, you would hardly find it so palatable a Piece: For really, Sir, I am afraid his Sophistry is as much out of your learn'd Sphere, as your Divinity (you are pleas'd to say) is out of mine, else you would not be such over-passionate Admirers of that Greatest of Carpers, and have such very humble Thoughts of the little, envious (and therefore scandalous Ones) his Answerers; but possible, your *Cambridge* Opinion of that Stage-Critick, may, like the rest of your Learning, be confin'd, as you call it, to your own Meridian, and then

MRS ELIZABETH BARRY (1658-1713)

you cannot do yourselves, nor the World more Justice, than to keep them both amongst you, especially if your Opinion and Learning are both of a Piece.

I am,

Your most humble Servant,

Gabriel Ballam.

P.S. Mr. Congreve's Answer is come out, wherein he proves Mr. Collier to be a very honest Man, by his false and imperfect Citations, and his becoming Assurance, in Charging him with his own Nonsense: All this is very plain, and fully proved, with mild, yet forceable Arguments. As to Mr. Dennis, I must be silent, for I have not yet read him.[33]

The next letter to Gabriel, although not dated, probably written c.1699, was from critic and dramatist, John Dennis. Dennis was one of the leading figures on the London literary scene though he eventually fell out with many of his contemporary greats, withdrawing from city life in 1704. The reasons for thinking that Dennis's letter might have been penned in 1699 are regarding his references to the *Play-house* and *Italians Voice,* as during that year his play/opera *Rinaldo and Armida* was performed at Lincoln's Inn Fields and printed in the same year; a strange choice

---

33 A Pacquet from Will's: Or a New Collection of Original Letters on several subjects;...Written and collected by several hands. London. Printed for Sam. Briscoe, and sold by John Nutt near Stationers-Hall, 1701. pp. 43-45

Gabriel Ballam's Friends

for Dennis as he was one of the most damning critics of opera of his day.

Dennis's letter to Gabriel Ballam, with particular reference to Gabriel's mistress at the playhouse:

To Mr. Gabriel——

Dear——
Though it seems hast a mind to pass for a Wit, by the very same means that *Æsop's Jack-Daw* thought fit to set up for a *Beaux*. (By the way I must tell you, that the Transformation of Beau to Wit, has something more of the Miracle in it, than the change of *Jack-Daw* to *Beau*) Yes, B——, with borrow'd Plumes hast thou imp'd thy Wings. But I took more particular notice of a couple, that were plucked from a certain Bird of Night; which if we give Credit to *W*—— the Owner is a very filthy obscene Animal; from which ominous Creature, may Heav'n defend us Mortals, that is, we in the Country here, call him *Bell*, but the Gods, that is, those in *Covent-Garden*, have named him *Break-a-day*. But it is time to begin to speak plain English, for you, if I am not mistaken, pretend to know other language: But then, as you have writ for the Witty Club, the Witty Club may understand for you. I look upon your last to be the Act and Deed of them all. And you shall henceforward be Secretary to them, as *Julian* was to their Mistresses. Tho' I must tell you by the way, that the Affection which some of them show for the Muses, is not unlike that merry Passion, which

MRS ELIZABETH BARRY (1658-1713)

put the little French parson into an amorous Fit for the Queen. Return them all Thanks, in my Name, for the Honour they have done me, in offering to admit me, in my Absence, a Member of their Noble Society. But, *Domine, non sum Dignas:* However, I think my self obliged to make them as extraordinary a compliment, as the *Morocco* Ambassador would have thought himself engaged to return the University of *Oxford*, if in the midst of their extream Civility, they had offered to make him *D.D.* But to speak to that part of your Letter which concerns yourself: I do not wonder, that you go to the Play-house only for the sake of your Mistress; but methinks, at the Music-meeting the Italians Voice might have Charms for you. But as you go thither too, you say, only for the sake of your Mistress, I will believe, to oblige you, that she does not go for the Eunuch's. Now I go to your Comedy here, purely for the Comedy sake, which is a Politic Country Club; and partly for the Musick sake I go to our Musick-meeting, which is a pack of shrill-mouth'd Beagles for Trebles, and a pack of deepmouth'd Bumpkins for Bases. And whenever our Consort begins, half the Men in *Bucks*, in spite of their Souls, are our Audience. Once more I salute the Witty Club; tell them, that they little deserve that Name, if they have not more Wit, than to take any thing ill I have said. Assure them, that I know how to respect their good Qualities, and that I shall endeavour to set off their Bad, which is a Friend's Part.

Gabriel Ballam's Friends

I am,

Dear———,

Yours, &c.

Postscript,
In your first Letter you gave me notice of some Gentlemen who designed to write to me. The Post before that, I had a very Witty Letter from one of them: it is no hard matter to guess that it was from Mr. *Wycherly.* But *Ch———* Wit, if he sent any, either went astray, or came short. Who should wonder at either?[34]

The letter from Wycherley to which Dennis refers is more than likely a letter dated the 1st of December 1694 which, in a postscript, makes reference to Gabriel: *Bal———says his ill Looks proceed rather for want of your Company, than for having had that of this Mistress.* A transcription will be found later in this work.

Here is Gabriel's reply to Dennis's letter, with further references to a lady of his acquaintance of *very great quality,* together with mention of a mistress *who has lately had 'em,* i.e. the smallpox.

Mr. Gabriel B———'s *Answer to Mr.* John D———; *to be left at* Will's *Coffee-house.*

---

34 A Pacquet from Will's: Or a New Collection of Original Letters on several subjects;...Written and collected by several hands. London. Printed for Sam. Briscoe, and sold by John Nutt near Stationers-Hall, 1701. pp. 46-48.

MRS ELIZABETH BARRY (1658-1713)

Yesterday I receiv'd a Letter from you, where you suspect the Rabble to other hand in my Letter; but you may assure your self it is not so, for I writ both mine in my Closet, and no body has seen 'em but your self; I do not say this to value myself upon two frivolous Letters, but that I would not have you suspect the Rabble of so much Dullness: indeed both yours I have shown to the Rabble (as you call 'em) or rather the Witty Club; and I have shown 'em to some of the Grave Club, and to some who are neither of the * Rabble nor grave Club, but both; and upon my word, they like 'em as well as I do. Since I writ to you, I have happen'd upon an Intreague with a Woman of very great Quality, (there's a Subject for your next Letter) which makes me up so much, that I have hardly time to eat: so you must not expect so just an Answer to your Letter (by reason of the length) as I would have done, had I been at liberty; so I hope you will excuse me: Our Correspondence hitherto methinks, looks as if we were seasoning a Sallad between us: I am for softning it with Oil, and you are still souring it with vinegar. (But pardon me) reflecting upon your last, if I dress the remaining part of my Letter according to your own Pallat. You hit me in the Teeth of having but one Language, which I am very well contented with, for I fear more Tongues than one would make me vain like other Folks, and so much Knowledge as you have, distract me; but if I can make a shift to write a Letter with indifferent Sense and good Breeding, (a thing harder to come by, than Latin or Greek,) I shall ne'er have occasion to doubt whether the Rabble's Wit shall take anything ill of me, whenever I shall write to 'em; which I am sure they do not of you, because they hold that Satyr (in its strictest Sense) is the incurable Disease of your Mind; tho' an essential Part of the witty and learned Mr. D——, and becomes you just as well as the Marks of the Small-Pox does a certain Mistress of mine, who has lately had 'em, which tho' it does not set her off at all, yet I am resolved to fancy her as much as before, because she cannot help her Blemishes.

I am yours, &c.[35]

I am not purporting to say categorically that the mistress referred to in Gabriel's letter is Mrs. Barry, I having found no particular reference to her ever having had *the smallpox*. However, with her leaving to Gabriel one of her greatest assets, the Town Mills, it would appear a strongly supported surmise. And with Gabriel being the first legatee named in her will, he was obviously at the forefront of her mind during her fatal illness. In a report of Mrs. Barry's death in *Volume III of Dramatic Micellanies* by Thomas Davies, London, 1784, it is said; *Cibber relates, in his Apology, that Mrs. Barry died, of a fever, in the latter part of Queen Anne's reign; and judges, by this expression, in her last delirium—— 'Ha! Ha! And so they make us lords by dozens!*

---

35 A Pacquet from Will's: Or a New Collection of Original Letters on several subjects;...Written and collected by several hands. London. Printed for Sam. Briscoe, and sold by John Nutt near Stationers-Hall, 1701. pp. 49-50

MRS ELIZABETH BARRY (1658-1713)

—— *that it was about the time when twelve peers were created at once. The date of her epitaph, at Acton, is fixed two years after this extraordinary promotion. An actress, who was in London when Mrs. Barry died, assured me, many years since, that her death was owing to the bite of a favourite lap-dog, who, unknown to her, had been seized with madness.* We can assume from this statement, if true, that poor Mrs. Barry died from rabies, *a viral disease that causes inflammation of the brain in humans and other mammals,* and with reference to *in her last delirium* it would seem this was a likely scenario.

And then Dennis's reply to that letter:

To Mr. Gabriel B——

Dear Gabriel,
When thy last was written, thou hast put on the Lyon's Skin, and mad'st a wonderful comical Figure in it. But I did not think to incense thee, nor the rest of the Rabble, quite contrary I thought to divert you. You say, you take it ill, that I should upbraid you with understanding no Language but English. Why, what of Pagan Apprehension hast thou, *Gabriel?* The Devil a jot did I upbraid thee: Quite contrary, I commended thee for being willing to understand no Language but plain English: And that, as I take it, has quite a different Meaning. With what unreasonable Wights have I had to do! Who are offended at my Endeavour to please them, and take my Commendations for Injuries. I am accus'd, you say, of ill Breeding for that Letter.

Gabriel Ballam's Friends

Why, prethee, *Gabriel*, every Man has not had the Breeding that thou hast. I wish you had sent me the Names of the Sparks who would reconcile Punctilio to Satyr. It has been a damn'd inveterate Quarrel, and requires wise Mediators. But now I talk of Satyr, that you say is the Disease of some Peoples Minds. Alas, poor Devil! Thou do'st not know that it is a Maxim in Physick, that some Diseases show the Health, and Strength, and Vigour of the Party affected: If we believe *Hippocrates*, Hunger is a Disease; nay, Reason tells us the same thing: For, like other Distempers, it shows a Defect in Nature; but where it shows a Defect, it shows a Force too; and when that Disease is pretty acute, the Patient is sure to do well: I will let the Application alone; for in writing to one of thy communicative Spirit, a Man is sure to write to some body who can understand. But this I will say, that if satyr be a Disease, the acuter it is, the better. But why do I talk of Diseases to thee? For indeed, *Gabriel*, (without satyr) thou art no Physitian.

I am, &c.[36]

The letter dated the 1st of December 1694, to Mr. John Dennis from dramatist William Wycherley *(1641-1716)*:
To Mr. Dennis.

---

36 A Pacquet from Will's: Or a New Collection of Original Letters on several subjects;...Written and collected by several hands. London. Printed for Sam. Briscoe, and sold by John Nutt near Stationers-Hall, 1701. pp. 53-54.

MRS ELIZABETH BARRY (1658-1713)

 Dear Sir,
I Have received yours of the 20th of *November*, and am glad to find by it, that however your Friends are losers by your Absence from the Town, you are a Gainer by it; of your Health, which every one you have left behind you, (but *Ch*—) may be thought a Friend to; and the more each Man is your Friend, the more he is satisfy'd with your Absence, which thô it makes us Ill for want of you, makes you well for want of us: your taking no leave of me (which you would excuse) I take to be one of the greatest Kindnesses you ever shew'd me; for I could no more see a Departing Friend from the Town, than a Departing Friend from this Life; and sure 'tis as much kindness and good breeding to steal from our Friend's Society unknown to 'em, (when we must leave 'em to their Trouble) as it is to steal out of a Room, after a Ceremonious Visit, to prevent trouble to him, whom we would Oblige and Respect; so that your last Fault (as you call it) is like the rest of your Faults, rather an Obligation than an Offence, thô the greatest Injury indeed you can do your Friends, is to leave 'em against their Will, which you must needs do. You tell me you converse with me in my Writings I must confess then you suffer a great deal for me in my Absence, which (thô I would have you love me) I would not have you do; but for your truer Diversion, pray change my *Country-Wife* for a better of your own in the Country, and exercise your own Plain-Dealing

there, then you will make your Country Squire better Company, and your Parson more sincere in in your Company than his Pulpit, or in his Cups: But when you talk of Store of Delights you find in my *Plain-Dealer*, you cease to be one; and when you commend my *Country-Wife*, you never were more a Courtier; and I doubt not but you will like your next Neighbour's Country Wife better than you do mine, that you may pass your time, better than you can do with my Country-Wife; and like her Innocence more than her Wit, since Innocence is the better Bawd to Love; but enjoy my Wife and welcome in my Absence, I shall take it as civilly as a City Cuckold; I was sorry to find by you that your head ak'd whilst you writ me your Letter. Since I fear 'twas from reading my Works (as you call them) not from your own Writing, which never gave you Pain, thô it would to others to imitate it, I've given your Service to your Friends at the Rose, who since your absence own they ought not to go for the Witty Club, nor is *Wills* the Wits Coffee-House any more, since you left it, whose Society for want of yours is grown as Melancholly, that is as dull as when you left 'em a Nights, to their own Mother-Wit, their Puns, Couplets, or Quibbles; therefore expect not a Witty Letter from any of them, no more than from me, since they, nor I have conversed with you these three Weeks. I have no News worth sending you, but my next shall bring you what we have; in the mean time let me tell you (what I hope is no News to you) that your Absence is

MRS ELIZABETH BARRY (1658-1713)

more tedious to me, than a Quibbler's Company to you; so that I being sick yesterday, as I thought without any cause, reflected you were Forty or Fifty Miles off, and then found the reason of my Indisposition, for I cannot be well so far from you, who am

My Dear Mr. *Dennis*

Your obliged humble Servant, W. Wycherly.
London, Dec. 1. 94.

Postscript.
Pray pardon me that I have not sooner answer'd your Letter, for I have been very busie this last Week about Law Affairs, that is, very Dull and Idle, thô very Active. Your Friends of the Coffee-House and the *Rose,* whether Drunk or Sober, Good Fellows or Good Wits, show at least their Sense, by valuing you and yours, and send you all their Service; and never are more Wits, and less Poets that is, less Lyars, than when they profess themselves your Servants.
For News, *W*—lives Soberly, *Ch*—goes to bed Early; *D'Vrfy* sings now like a Poet, that is, without being ask'd: And all the Poets or Wits-at-Wills, since your departure, speak well of the Absent. *Bal*—says his ill Looks proceed rather for want of your Company, than for having had that of this Mistress; even the Quibblers and

Gabriel Ballam's Friends

Politicians, have no Double-meaning when they speak well of you.[37]

Another rather interesting piece regarding Gabriel, written in 1691, is a five page *Epistle Dedicatory* to him and signed E. Settle. The splendidly named poet and playwright, Elkanah Settle *(1648-1724)* was a friend of John Wilmot, 2nd Earl of Rochester. The Earl encouraged him much in his writings. The work in which the Epistle appeared was Settle's *The compleat memoirs of the life of that notorious impostor Will. Morrell, alias Bowyer, alias Wickham, &c. Who died at Mr. Cullen's the bakers in the strand, Jan. 3. 1691/2.* Gabriel was only eighteen at the time of the dedicatory and apparently had already become a popular figure among his contemporaries. As Elkanah says of Gabriel, *You have that Air of Sweetness and obliging Temper, a Conversation so grateful, as renders you the Favourite even of Both Sexes...You are so great a Cherisher of the Muses and the Stage,...* With these flattering sentiments, it wouldn't be hard to imagine Mrs. Barry, the celebrated actress, being enamoured by such a delicious young man, fifteen years her junior, paying court to her. If the likes of Rochester and Etherege had found Mrs. Barry an attractive and sexually alluring woman, there is no reason why young Gabriel wouldn't have been of a like mind, he being, as it appears, *a Cherisher of the Muses and the Stage.*

---

37 Letters upon several occasions written by and between Mr. Dryden, Mr. Wycherly, Mr.----, Mr. Congreve, and Mr. Dennis, published by Mr. Dennis with a new translation of select letters of Monsieur Voiture. London: Printed for Sam. Briscoe, 1696. pp.24-27
https://quod.lib.umich.edu/e/eebo/A35671.0001.001?view=toc

MRS ELIZABETH BARRY (1658-1713)

Settle's play *Empress of Morocco* (1673) was performed for King Charles II at Whitehall, and was a great success. It was during this time that Lord Rochester and Mrs. Barry became lovers. Could Settle's friendship with Gabriel have been a contributing factor to him later being introduced, and befriending Mrs. Barry?

The Epistle Dedicatory to Gabriel Balam *[Ballam]*:

Gabriel Balam, Esq
SIR,

A Fair Name in the Frontispiece of a Book, is by long Custom reckoned as Essential a part of it, as a *Portico* is of a Temple. And yet as Panegyricks are their common Furniture, Dedication is the nicest part of Writing.

For though the Honest Poet, like the Faithful Painter, draws not beyond the Life, 'tis still but a sort of Labour lost. For as Modesty is the Finishing Stroke to the Compleat Gentleman, That Patron that is the most worthy of Praise, is the least fond of it.

And if we stretch into that nauseous Extream of Flattery, the Panegyrick is turn'd into a Libel, by exposing what we pretend to praise.

The Epistle Dedicatory

'Tis true, the Pretence of Dedications, is the borrowed Protection a piece of Scribble receives from the Noble Patron, under whose Umbrage 'tis usher'd into the World. When, alas, a great Patron is no more a Protection to a dull Book, than a Cesar's Face to a leaden Shilling. Wit and

Sense stand only upon their own Legs, and go no farther than their own intrinsick Merit carries them. The World, at least the Judicious part of it, is not to be so cheated. There's no passing off that false Coin for which every Man of Sense has both a Scales and a Touch-stone. Wit runs the Fate of *Belteshazzar*: The *[Mene Tekel]* is certainly written over our Heads, if we are once weigh'd and found too Light.

But supposing some favour'd Author, cherish'd by the Smiles of a Noble or Generous Patron, takes this occasion (for that's the fairest Dedicatory pretext) of avowing his Gratitude to the whole World for such signal Obligations; yet this publick Acknowledgment of past Favours, looks very suspiciously like a Design of drawing on of new ones too: So that to sum up the Cause, the Brotherhood of the Quill, if they would fairly unmask, should plainly tell the World, that there's a private Gratification goes along with the publick Acknowledgment. For Men make Dedications as Votaries make Thanksgivings: The bent Knee is not wholly for Blessings receiv'd; but for some little Continuation too of the kind descending Smiles.

And, Faith, now I am playing the Tell-troth, and making thus bold with the Poetick Fraternity; this common Fault amongst them may well be excused: For to Apologize for the Muses in their own Native Dialect, I need but quote a Stanza in *Gondibert*.

MRS ELIZABETH BARRY (1658-1713)

> O hireless Science; and of all alone
> The Liberal! Meanly the rest each State
> With Pension treats: But this depends of none;
> Whose Worth they reverently forbear to rate.

If Poor Poetry is put to such hard Shifts (for maugre our *Gondibert's* fair Flourish, that's the plain English) to be so wholly unprovided for, that the Muses have neither Lands nor Livings annex'd to their Foundation, but are wholly supported by Goodness and Favour; whilst all other Studies, whether in the Long or Black Robe, have their Preferments, as warm Gowns, soft Furs, fat Glebes, and fruitful Crops, and what not: And Poetry, as much as 'tis charg'd with Fiction, yet, like Truth, goes almost naked: Under these Melancholly Circumstances it may well be permitted some Grains of Allowance, as an Unhappy Dependant upon Courtesie.

But whilst I am thus plain in correcting Faults abroad, I ought to look at home, as having a much weaker Plea for my own Dedication, when being so altogether a Stranger to you, I dare be guilty of this Presumption. This indeed I ought to have consider'd: But when I find the Ingenious every day making their Court to you, and the more eminent Priests of *Apollo*, the more successful and no less deservingly so, all assiduous Suitors to your Favour; so many fair Examples are that Warrant for my Ambition, that I lay hold of any Occasion, tho at a farther distance, of making one of the Train.

You have that Air of Sweetness and obliging Temper, a Conversation so grateful, as renders you the Favourite even of Both Sexes.

But if I proceed to sum up your fair Character, I shall transgress the Laws I have laid down, and offend that Modesty, as has an Ear too tender for that Subject. Not to enlarge therefore upon your other Merits, 'tis sufficient, You are so great a Cherisher of the Muses and the Stage, that that single Virtue alone has encourag'd me to the Confidence of this Address.

All I have truly to blush at, is the slenderness of the Present, this inconsiderable Trifle I offer you. However, as the Crow presented to Cesar, be pleased to give it the same favourable Acceptance, as indeed (like that poor Crow) saluting you with the same [Hayle] only with more Zeal, and tend'ring you the humble Obedience of

    SIR,

Your most Devoted Servant

E. SETTLE.[38]

Mrs. Barry's acquaintances, and indeed her lovers, all seem to have been people of education, wit and substance, and

---

38 The compleat memoirs of the life of that notorious impostor Will. Morrell, alias Bowyer, alias Wickham, &c. Who died at Mr. Cullen's the bakers in the strand, Jan. 3. 1691. Elkanah Settle. London: Printed for Abel Roper and E. Wilkinson at the Black Boy over against St. Dunstan's Church in Fleet-street, 1694. https://quod.lib.umich.edu/e/eebo/A59303.0001.001/1:2?rgn=div1;view=fulltext

MRS ELIZABETH BARRY (1658-1713)

with a mutual respect for her. Some of her earlier lovers, it is believed, were; John Wilmot, 2nd Earl of Rochester; Sir George Etherege *(c.1636-c.1692)*; Charles Dering *(1657-1719)*; and Henry Goring *(1646-1685)*. Goring was tragically killed by Dering in Mrs. Barry's dressing room, this believed to be at Drury Lane; these men, who had apparently been former lovers of Mrs. Barry, were both under the influence of drink and caused a fracas in her room after the stage play was ended. Dering was subsequently arrested for murder, but soon was free on bail. The outcome of the Coroner's inquest was the lesser verdict of manslaughter, then so often the case with the privileged wealthy.

It is reported that politician Henry St. John, 1st Viscount St. John *(1652-1742)* might have also been a lover of Mrs. Barry. If this be true, not only had Countess Anne Wilmot's son Rochester been Barry's lover, but her nephew may have been her lover too! This surely would have been too much for Anne to stomach. Were Mrs. Barry's relationships with these men not just born of a sexual attraction, but possibly of an intellectual nature too? Food for thought.

EPILOGUE

Mrs. Elizabeth Barry was certainly a great celebrity of her day, and was revered by many for her acting prowess but, as can be seen, she had acquired many friends and acquaintances not just in the world of theatre. These friends of Mrs. Barry were from all walks of life including; those of the Court; titled folk of eminent families; artists, writers, poets and dramatists; and ordinary people too.

To have known and befriended such a wide variety of people, Mrs. Barry must have been an intelligent and amiable person.

One of Elizabeth's closest friends was the fresh-faced Anne Bracegirdle, the darling of the stage. There was never any rivalry between these two actresses who respected each other throughout their careers and long after. They each had a similar background, of a family experiencing hard times, with a consequence of the children finding their own way in the world. Was this the mutual catalyst that prompted Elizabeth and Anne's affection for each other?

Elizabeth's freedom and independence, on and off the Stage, might have been a reason for her never marrying, although I can imagine she would have had plenty of offers. And who knows, in her years of retirement, had she lived long enough, she might well have taken the opportunity of a companion husband in her dotage. But I feel that would never have been her style, she having lived such a celebrated life of fame as a single, independent woman.

And probably given time, with which tragically she had not been blessed, she might have, during her residence in

MRS ELIZABETH BARRY (1658-1713)

Acton's sweet air, written her memoirs. And what a best seller that would have been, then and now. One can only imagine the fascinating contents such a work would have held; from her presumed humble beginnings in her role as a lady's maid to her celebrated roles on the Stage and from her purported string of lovers to her supposedly mercenary reputation so maliciously and undeservedly penned by ruthless satirists. But what other things might we have read in such memoirs? I believe we would have learned of Mrs. Barry's good education, for she could no doubt read and write as well as anyone. She had the gift to memorize her lines of all the many characters she performed, which would have been no easy task. Could she in her later years, as a woman of some wealth and good taste, possessing fine clothes and a well furnished house, have entertained people of quality and refinement including wits, dramatists, poets, artists and musicians? Or probably, being in the media so to speak, would she have enjoyed solace away from the crowded theatre, with a handful of special friends where she could relax in their company? Her retirement to Acton would seem to suggest the latter.

We could speculate forever what would and could have been had the gifted Mrs. Elizabeth Barry survived into real old age and outlived many of her contemporaries. Had she died in 1748, at the age of ninety, with her close friend Anne Bracegirdle dying that year at the age of seventy-seven, one contemplates what reminiscences those two stalwarts of the London Stage would have enjoyed sat by a warming winter's fire, sparking memories by the dozen … they calling for their pattens and clogs.

Now I talk of players, tell Mr Chute that his friend Bracegirdle breakfasted with me this

Epilogue

morning. As she went out, and wanted her clogs, she turned to me and said - 'I remember at the playhouse they used to call - Mrs. Oldfield's chair! Mrs. Barry's clogs! And Mrs. Bracegirdle's pattens!'[39]

---

39 *Tragedy Queens of the Georgian Era by John Fyvie London. 1908. pp 32 -33*

Printed in Great Britain
by Amazon